The Ground Kisser

Thanh Dương Boyer

And

Lisa Worthey Smith

Biographies & memoirs: Historical: Asia: india & South Asia: Vietnam
Biographies &memoirs: historical: Asia: India and South Asia: survival
Biographies & Memoirs: Survival: immigration.

ISBN-13: 978-1-947523-36-4
ISBN-10: 1-947523-36-8

Dedication

I dedicate my story, my life, and this book
to honor the Lord Jesus Christ,
and offer my heartfelt gratitude to our veterans,
especially the Vietnam War Veterans.

Acknowledgements

This list in no way reflects all who have influenced my life, but I do want to recognize and give special thanks to the following people;

My sponsors and other people who helped me when I first came to the United States, including:
George and Maria VanKirk, Larry and Kay Burlingame, Lucille Morrison, Frances Andrews, The people of St. Paul Catholic Church, The people of First Presbyterian Church, Janet Waggoner (ESL teacher), and Doris Todd (3rd grade teacher).

Immigration official:
Frank

My family members including:
My parents, Tu My and Phuong Duong, my adopted parents (John's parents), John Boyer Sr. and Sue Boyer, Loan and Paul McAllister, Thu and Randy Smith, Xinh and Phat Tran, Duyen and Xuong Trieu, Tham and Thuy Duong, Todd and Leslie Boyer, Thang and Be Duong (my aunt and uncle), Hung Duong, Minh Duong, Buu Duong, and Thom Duong (my aunt in Switzerland).

My many friends, especially:
David and Pam Chandler, Lynne and Dave Chambers, Rick and Wendy Dillon, Nathan and Susan Johnson, Chuck and Maureen Driessnack, Glen and Cindy Yates, Johnny and Greta Smith, Tom and Joani

Strickland, Blake and Sandra Rymer, Adrian Shrider, Faron Davis, Congregation of Austinville Church of God, Brother Harold Coomer, The Congregation of Rivertree Church, my Twisted Sisters Tennis Team, along with many others who have prayed for and encouraged me along the way.

My fabulous sister,
Lisa Worthey Smith for her incredible writing skills.

My husband,
John. You always believe in me and remain my biggest cheerleader. You are my "white" in shining armor!

Our children,
Katherine and JB Boyer. There isn't anything that I won't do for you. I love you to the moon and back.

Reviews

"Gripping story. I have held my breath so many times I am nearly blue! Made my heart pound and weep."
Eva Marie Everson,
Award-winning author,
President Word Weavers International

~~~

"This book had me from the first paragraph. I started reading it while at a Christian Writers Retreat in at the beautiful Blue Lake Methodist Conference Center in Alabama. When I got home, I pulled it back out and read every night.

Heartbreaking but full of hope, *The Ground Kisser* by Thanh Duong Boyer with Lisa Worthey Smith, is the amazing true story of Thanh's escape with her younger sister from Vietnam after the fall of Saigon. Her parents had to make the agonizing decision to put their two oldest daughters on a boat and watch them slip away toward the South China Sea where they would encounter pirates, survive a storm and wind up on a refugee island in Indonesia.

But the story has a happy ending. Thanh made it to America and then worked hard to make sure her entire immediate family would all come to Alabama, the place she called home after surviving so many horrors of war.

At a time when our nation seems constantly divided and full of hatred and fear, this book brought me a new hope. God is in control and we are all blessed because our brave Vietnam veterans fought against the same horrors that Thanh encountered on her perilous journey. With strength and courage beyond her young years, Thanh did everything she could to survive and

thrive in America. Read this book and then pass it on to someone who needs encouragement and hope. You will not be disappointed."
Lenora Worth,
NY Times bestselling author

~~~

"This book should be required reading for all students—for all Americans.

It is said that 'all life is comparison.' When people compare standards of living, we realize how fortunate we are. This book puts an exclamation mark on what it means to live in America."
The Honorable Tommy M. Battle,
Mayor of Huntsville, AL

~~~

"*The Ground Kisser* is a sure cure for anyone jaded by privileged American life. Thanh Boyer's story of escaping Communist oppression in Vietnam as a child and suffering through unimaginable physical and emotional misery on her way to the American dream should be required reading for every high school student in America.

It is a vivid true tale of suffering, love, family commitment, redemption and, finally, the realization of the best part of America's promise.

God Bless Thanh and her amazing courage!"
Richard Judy,
Author of *THRU: An Appalachian Trail Love Story*

~~~

"As a clinical psychologist, I continue to counsel veterans and have counseled South Vietnamese families who came to the United States before the fall of South Vietnam. Leaving my unit, the country, and the people we did our best to protect, I am grateful for all we did together. The South Vietnamese people, both military and civilian, did their part to protect us with information, support, and bringing us into their lives.

In her book, *The Ground Kisser*, Thanh Boyer writes of the many challenges and tragedies with the fall of the South Vietnamese government. Back here, I experienced the story of the fall of Saigon with innermost sadness. Deeply ingrained in me are memories of Vietnamese people—the families, the children, and the orphanages—as well as the commitments, sacrifices, and casualties of American soldiers.

War and its effects never leave us. Pain is one thing we all share in common and is, in many ways, our best teacher.

Thanh's story is for each of us who understand and appreciate the value of the human spirit to overcome adversity, the importance of a helping hand, and the faith to endure. She puts a human face on the heartbreaking sacrifices families make in hopes that their children will have a better life.

She leaves behind her parents and siblings and endures a treacherous journey from South Vietnam to America where she is met with generosity and hope. She and her husband continue to give back, helping family, neighbors, and community, and expressing deep gratitude for our country and our veterans.

Thank you for your survival, for never giving up,

and for sharing your story."

Terrence J. Johnson, Ph.D., Clinical Psychologist
US Army 134th Assault Helicopter Company
Specialist 4 Phu Hiep, South Vietnam 1968-69

~~~

"I was intrigued and mesmerized by Thanh's life story after hearing her speak. Now that I have read the in-depth accounting of her life and her humble testimony of God's love, I am in awe.

I am honored and proud to have nominated her for one of DAR's highest awards, the Americanism Award. She not only won at the state level, but was the recipient of the 2016 National Americanism Medal. This is a must-read book."

Penny Sumners
Honorary Regent of Twickenham Town Chapter of the DAR

Foreword

by John Boyer, Thanh's husband

Thanh was given the name, "Ground Kisser," by legendary radio talk-show host, Barry Farber, when he heard her story many years ago. Mr. Farber described a Ground Kisser as the kind of immigrant that gets off the plane and immediately kisses the ground of his adopted country. Ground Kissers understand that while it's not perfect, the United States of America represents something unique in human history.

The radical idea that individual human rights are God given and that government derives its right from the people and not the other way around has changed the world for the better. As Americans, the enormous richness and comfort of our lives often lull us to sleep. That was true for me.

Over the years, we have met so many Vietnamese people like Thanh with amazing stories. Most of them are much like our grandparents who lived through the depression and the great wars; they simply live their lives and don't talk about it much.

We believe that these stories should be told, so that people can understand what it really means to live in a free country. To escape tyranny. Thanh knows what tyranny is like and she realizes how special, almost sacred, her obligation is to share her story.

I have heard that chance favors the prepared mind, and Thanh's mind is well-suited for the role she has played in life. She is tough—some might call the trait stubborn—but she rounds it out with an amazing sense of humor. At times, she is simply a force of nature, with more willpower than anyone I've ever met. But most of the time, she is a happy and positive person, who simply loves to serve the people in her community.

For the second time in my life, I am in Costa Rica. It is only fitting that I write the foreword to Thanh's book from here. Over thirty years ago, I was here in Costa Rica, on a mission trip and had a life changing experience. Like Thanh, it wasn't a Damascus-road vision with God speaking to me; it was more of a friendly thump in the back of the head.

One of nineteen men from my church who came down to build a house, I spent my week sweating with a pick and shovel in a small mountain village. While I was sweating, I was thinking.

At the time, I was engaged to a smart, pretty, blond girl from my home in Alabama. She was everything I ever wanted. Except, I realized, she wasn't. Being disconnected in a foreign country made me remember a long-forgotten memory from my childhood. My younger self had imagined myself married to an Asian. I didn't know the details; I just knew that the path I was on wasn't the right one.

When I returned home, I called off the engagement. Not even a year after that, Thanh and I were introduced, and the rest is history. Things were tough at times, but they always felt right. It was like seeing a perfect sunset or accidently making a hole in one. Things just happened the right way at the right time.

When you read this book, you might get the impression that Thanh and I are near-perfect people. We aren't perfect; there just isn't enough room in a book to share the stupid things we've done. I don't even consider myself a good man, but I've done some good things. I have failed many times as a husband, father, and person. Thanh has failed many times as well.

What we did do, however, is put our faith in God when we needed to the most. Then we got caught up in something that He wanted to do.

~~~

One last thing. Over the years I've kept a running list of the funny things Thanh and her family have said accidently. Her spoonerisms have given all of us a lot of enjoyment over the years. If you'd like to see a few, please see the "Thanhisms" near the end of this book and visit the website www.TheGroundKisser.com for more.

John Boyer
December 2018
Cahuita, CR

Preface

By Thanh Duong Boyer

I spent most of my life in North Alabama. I'm a southerner by choice, and I love it. But the first twelve years of my life I was in Vietnam, during the civil war, the war with Pol Pot of Cambodia, and under Communism. I know about hard times.

Over the last twenty-five years, folks have told me over and over I need to write it all down. I need to tell my story. I need to write a book. So why write the book now?

Well, you could say I have had a transformation. Not quite like Paul on the Damascus Road by any means, but one that caught my full attention and caused my complete surrender.

I came to realize that my life journey is a gift from the Almighty. Yes, some folks may not see it as a gift, but for me it is. It was revealed to me through many days of being still and in prayer that I was saved from war, piracy, starvation, and disease for a reason. And the reason has nothing to do with me—*imagine that*—but has everything to do with Him, Who gave me this life.

Dear readers: Know that I am in no way in my comfort zone. Doing this has stretched me to the max. I would rather clean a public toilet.

Why such resistance? Because *fear* is my enemy. Like those who have been through something like The Great Depression, it is so painful to relive. So yes, out of my selfishness, I would rather not have dredged up the pain buried deep down in me.

But then God revealed to me that healing for others

can take place through the telling of my story. So, you see it isn't about me at all. I am not doing this for notoriety, money, or fame. As a matter of fact, the proceeds of my book go to some of my favorite charities—Abandoned Little Angels, Salvation Army, and a veteran's organization.

I have two main goals for telling my story. The first is that it help bring closure and healing from the Vietnam War to our veterans. Our Vietnam vets need to know that they are appreciated, and this naturalized citizen is forever grateful to them for their sacrifices.

My second goal is that those who are going through hardship know that they can persevere, and that all things are possible with God.

I hope you enjoy this book. Go thank a veteran. I like to show my gratefulness to our veterans by buying their meals, whether anonymous or in person.

Blessings,
Thanh

Cast of Characters

My Family and Other Names within My Story.

You will find photographs of many of these people and places at the end of the book.

My Grandparents

Liêm Dương \Li-am Yuun\ My paternal grandfather. I called him Ông Nôi \Auhm No-ey\
Ba Nôi \Baah No-ey\ My paternal grandmother.
Nguyen Van Thiet \Ween vaan Dit\ My maternal grandfather. I called him Ông Ngoai \Auhm Why\
Ba Ngoai \Baah Why\ My maternal grandmother.

My Parents

My Tân Dương \Mee Taan Yuun\ My father
Ba \Baah\ Dad
Phương Nguyễn \Fuun Wee\ My mother
Mẹ \May-ah\ Mom

Their Children

Thanh \Taahn\ rhymes with John. Born in 1967
Loan \Laahn\ rhymes with John. Born in 1969
Thu \Too\ Born in 1970
Xinh \Sing\ without the g. Born in 1972
Duyên \Ying\ Born 1973
Thăm \Tom\ Born in 1974

My Aunts and Uncles and Their Children

Thang \Tain\ My uncle. I called him Dương Mười \Yuun Mu-ai\. He married my father's sister

Bé \Be-a\ My aunt. My father's sister. I called her Cô Mười \Kho Mu-ai\ literally "Aunt

Ten"because of her position as the ninth child in my father's family.

Their Sons

Hung \Home\
Minh \Mun\
Buu \Bou\

~~~

Ông Bi \Auhm Bee\ My uncle. Literally "Mr. Bi."

Thom \Tum\ My aunt. My father's sister. I called her Cô Sau \Kho Sa-uu\ literally "Aunt Six" of my father's siblings.

Their daughter

Hue \Whey\ Born in KuKu Island refugee camp.

~~~

Ông Phồn Tam \Auhm Fone Tom\ Mr. Phon, the boat owner.

Chapter 1

1975
Tân Châu, An Giang, Vietnam

I willed my eyes to look in the direction of the chalkboard in front of me, but my mind drifted to my beloved market a few blocks away. The words of my second-grade teacher faded into the background as my daydream transported me away. In my dream, I strolled the market—the way it used to be—with the vibrant smell and feel of fresh melons, the sound of squawking chickens, and the lively banter of vendors bargaining with customers. I felt the cool water on my fingertips when they tickled the top of the pools swirling with live fish.

My brain rattled back into reality when the blast rang through the open windows of the school and pierced my eardrums to the jawbone. My hands reached up to protect my ears but diverted and grabbed the long wooden desktop before me while the floor shuddered. Directly in front of me, my teacher leaned over her desk and gripped the top edges, her mouth and eyes open wide. The building shook. Rubble from the walls and ceiling stung my arms and face. A thick cloud whooshed through the open windows and engulfed us with putrid, metallic smoke.

When the floor settled, I released my grip on the desk and squirmed out from behind it. A series of coughs fought to defend my lungs. I raised one arm, covered my mouth, then set my legs on the mission they practiced many times before: move outside to the bomb trenches. Before the teacher could steady herself, take a breath and yell out the familiar *"Chạy! Chạy chạy nhanh lên,"* I had already headed toward the door.

Once outside, my lungs begged for clean air, but found only more dust and blue smoke. Instead of diving into the trenches, I lowered my arm and tried to gain my bearings. Everything drifted in slow motion, out of focus, out of place. I blinked hard to clear the grit from my eyes and forced them to focus through the swirling cloud, yet nothing familiar came into view.

Through the smoke, the outline of our schoolyard gate materialized, and I passed through it to the street out front. Before entering the gate earlier that day, I stood in that same spot and waved a cheery morning greeting to the family who lived across the street, who responded with big smiles and waves. This sweet family made tasty little snacks for us to buy before we headed home from school every day. Now, where their home should have been, flames spewed from a vast crater filled with flaming metal and wood.

My heart bullied its way up my throat and pounded against my airway, leaving me no room to breathe, much less produce a sound. Screams of those next to

13

me sounded muffled and distant. I covered my mouth while ash and rubble peppered me, but still gagged from the dust, smoke, and the sight before me. I bent over, hands to knees, and braced myself as a wave of nausea retched in me, but only produced a few deep coughs.

Underfoot, odd multi-colored debris littered this strange landscape and grabbed my attention. My feet tugged against my flip-flops that stuck to the overheated ground, while I made my way toward the flickering fragments. My curious fingers reached down to inspect an intriguing piece of shimmering blue metal. In response to the instantaneous sizzle, my fingers slung the angry metal far away. I plunged my burning fingers into my mouth. My parents had been right about burning shell fragments after all. I sucked my scorched fingers, stood in place, and looked in all directions for something—anything—familiar.

My classmates and teachers shuffled with the same blank faces and ash-covered clothing. Teachers wandered from child to crying child, patted their shoulders, leaned over them, and mouthed unheard words of comfort. Their eyes skipped around, counted heads, and surveyed damage without answering what we wanted to know.

I took in the scene, the sting of tears sneaking up unbidden. I couldn't let them see me cry. I wouldn't. I turned my head and faked an extra cough to disguise a stray sob. I had to be brave so I could get home to my family.

Stop.

Think.

Breathe.

We didn't live far from school; my father had surely heard the blast. He would come for me. I forced my eyes to look away from the devastation around me and search for him. He would come, and then everything would be okay.

One step at a time, I navigated through the searing metal shards and the thickest part of the smoke and debris. My eyes squinted to focus in the direction of the road leading home. Finally, part of the road came into view and I set a path toward it. My flip-flops slapped my heel after every tug-of-war step over and around the flickering metal. Only two or three blinks later, I spotted a familiar dust cloud moving furiously toward me, led by my father's motorcycle.

I lifted both hands and crossed them high over my head and called out "Ba," but my voice echoed from a deep well, far away. Tears welled up and threatened to break through. I knew he would come. Time finally ticked at its proper pace and my heart lowered back into my chest.

Ba spotted me and skillfully maneuvered the bike over the rough road in my direction. My little legs put all their effort into the race to meet him. My flip-flops couldn't keep up and stayed behind.

He pulled up beside me and lowered one foot to the ground while I saddled up into my spot behind his seat, wrapped my arms around him, then secured my feet on the footrests. He picked up his foot, made a smooth half-loop, and maneuvered us on the road toward home. Home. Our home. Our family. Together.

We bounced in sync with the bumps in the road. The bobbing encouraged productive coughs that transformed into full sobs. I had survived. I would go home today.

Safe, I closed my eyes and let hot tears slip out. My trembling body and racing heart eased as I leaned on his strong back and we passed the familiar businesses and streets I loved so dearly.

Almost home, I reminded my lungs to slow down. Breathe in. Breathe out. My deafened ears finally picked up the sound of gravel crunching under our motorcycle. The block where we lived remained intact and undamaged. The whole row of terraced homes stood tall in a neat row with ours at the end.

Ba slowed to park the bike and my foggy eyes cleared at the sight of our home clad in stucco, topped with a metal roof. I sighed out a huge lungful of soot and replaced it with a clean breath of peace into my heart. The double accordion-style metal doors pushed far to each side, welcoming us with wide open arms.

He tilted the bike to one side and held the handlebars steady. I took the cue, planted one foot on the ground, kicked the other leg up and over the back of the bike, peeled myself from him and slid out of my seat, leaving his back smeared with soot and ash.

While he dismounted and secured the motorcycle, I brushed the dust from my clothes and feet and flicked off some of the tearstained grit from my face before I padded through the doorway—shoulders back and face set to brave and strong—Ba close behind. My embarrassed fingers curled inward toward my palm. No one needed to know about that right now.

Inside, our pointed coolie hats were still stacked neatly by the doorway. To the right, a trunk-like box served double-duty as both seating and storage for my parents' bedding. A small table and a few chairs anchored the opposite side, leaving an open walkway in the center.

Our Buddhist shrines sat unphased, cross-legged on their little table. One held smoldering incense in respect and remembrance of the dead. The other guarded our home from any evil that tried to enter. Family pictures that captured sweet moments in time smiled at me from the wall. Those were happy days. No smiles in my heart or on my face today.

I turned at the stairwell and made my way up the ladder-like wooden steps. Once alone in my room, I unfolded my hand and found blistered fingers. I should have listened to my parents' warning about the shell fragments.

I did listen to them.

I didn't obey them, but I listened.

Too late now. It would be much less painful to deal with the pain of the burns than to go through the shame of revealing my stubborn disobedience.

First task, clean off the ash. I dipped a galvanized scoop into the concrete basin to the left, drew out some water and splashed it on my face. The ash rinsed off, but the concrete dust held its ground. Deep cleaning required a washcloth. I grabbed one and soaked it in the water. My sore fingers moved out to the side to avoid the water, but I recruited two good fingers that could handle the twisting needed to wring some water out of the washcloth.

The first swipe dragged the residue across my skin like coarse sandpaper. I shuddered at the unexpected pain.

Deep breath.

No tears.

In silence I patted the washcloth over the grime, but nothing came off. I tried again, adding some light, tender strokes and found a few crumbs on the washcloth. Gradually the gentle swabs removed a layer at a time of the cinder-dust and still left my skin intact. Limb by limb, I continued the delicate wash and found no serious wounds. Once clean, I poured out a whole scoop of water over the top my head for a final shower to rinse away any residue of the day.

After I washed the stench of smoke from my skin, soot from my clothes, and tears from my face, I turned and caught a breeze from our window that cooled my tender skin. I ran my good fingers through my dripping wet hair and let the warm waft of air flow through it.

Outside the window on our balcony/patio, our freshly washed clothes danced lightly in the breeze while they dried. Did they not know? How could they possibly dance at such a time? Would I ever cleanse my mind of the scene I witnessed that day? Would there ever be a day when I danced in the breeze again, as they did?

~~~

As clean and dry as I could manage, I went back downstairs. At least with bombs this near to us, I wouldn't have to return to school that day. If I were lucky, the next either. When I passed by the "Dương Home" sign on the wall, I lifted my droopy shoulders and straightened my back a little taller—proud of our family name, our standing, and our home.

I tucked my feet under me, sat on the floor and watched my siblings play quietly around me, unaware of what had happened at school. The before-and-after pictures of the snack-maker family and their home replayed in my mind. My good fingers twirled the hem of my fresh shirt while I searched for them in every replay. Were their faces in the smoke? Maybe they stood to the side. Everyone looked the same covered with ash.

No matter how many times I reran the scene, I couldn't find them in the crowd. The clear image of the charred pit that displaced their home forced me to accept the truth. Tears rushed up. I blinked hard to force them back—only the weak agonize over the dead. I took a deep breath and sat in silent respect for the loss of the day, and the survival of the day. Incense would burn for the snack-makers in the morning.

Sundown arrived. We ate our meal. The crickets chirped their nighttime songs outside our open windows. Birds settled in the guava tree outside our balcony window to nest for the night. We pulled out the mosquito netting from its place and spread it out. My hands and feet went through the motions of all our usual activities.

My mind refused to comply. Over and over it replayed the image of the snack-makers waving and smiling at me for the last time, and the chaos of flames and smoke that took them away.

Would my normal ever include joy again? I tried to wash the scene away, or at least any telltale tears, with another shower before bedtime.

Chapter 2

Born into a family rich with tradition, I treasured the fascinating tales my grandfather told of his youth and his father, my great-grandfather, a highly respected medicine man in China. When illness or injury struck, people lined up at his door for a remedy. He listened to their complaints, formed a diagnosis, and mixed a blend of ingredients from herbs, tree bark, berries, animal parts and oils—yes, including snake oil—and a multitude of secret ingredients, with specific instructions for using them. Sometimes, he compounded them into a liniment to be applied to the skin. For other maladies he crushed and bagged a dried mixture to be boiled and taken as a healing tea.

My great-grandfather developed a "general good health" concoction with various roots, leaves, seeds, and berries that modern-day scientists agree have health benefits. He knew about these now-popular "health foods" long before any doctors knew how or why the ingredients worked. My father keeps a jar of this healthy brew on his kitchen counter at all times, and he considers it far better than processed vitamin pills.

When Communism replaced the empirical rule in China, my wise great-grandfather left. He and my great-grandmother traveled by boat from south China along the coast of North Vietnam, around the southern tip of South Vietnam and initially settled in the coastal town of Ha Tien, just south of the Cambodian border. From that western coast, they migrated about seventy-five miles inland to Tân Châu, AnGiang, Vietnam, in the vibrant Mekong delta, six miles south of Cambodia.

They left behind the fine porcelain dishes they dined from in China, and used old coconut shells along the way to hold their food—a minor tradeoff to live in freedom.

While they escaped one type of oppression in China, they encountered prejudice against people of Chinese ethnicity in Vietnam. My great-grandfather altered his last name from the Chinese "Ô", to a more Vietnamese-sounding name, finally settling on "Dương." Gradually, they won the confidence of their neighbors, started a business, and a family.

One of their children became my grandfather. I called him Ông Nội—literally "my father's father." My equally wise ông nội realized they were perfectly located to buy Cambodian silk at wholesale price, then retail it in Saigon. Situated on this natural transportation route, the Mekong practically begged for business opportunities. My grandfather capitalized on the idea, grew into a natural merchant, developed several businesses, and began a family of his own.

One of his sons, my father, ("Ba") joined him in the family businesses. When my generation came along, we worked alongside them. Mẹ ("Mom") and Ba welcomed me, their firstborn, into the world in 1967 with a champagne bath—a tradition in wealthy families. Four more daughters followed before my brother arrived and completed our family.

During my early years, Ông Nội's extended family worked together to nurture existing businesses and start more when opportunities arose. His business ventures included a bakery, a delicatessen, silk, and general merchandise, all within walking distance of his three-story home—my second home, and my playground.

From the boat dock behind Ông Nội's house, I had a front-row seat to the action along our Mekong. I dangled my feet off the edge and swished them back and forth in the cool river while the fishermen in long shallow boats cast their nets into the water and drew in abundant sparkling carp. They brought some of their catch into the market to be sold fresh that day. The remaining were butterflied and laid out on pallets of netting, strung across bamboo frames, to dry under the tropical sun.

Smaller boats brought baskets piled high with corn, peas, rice, and nuts. Many merchants in these canoe-type boats lined up side by side and sold their wares from boat to boat. Others brought their goods ashore to sell in our chợ trời, an open-air market.

From the front of Ông Nội's home, I relaxed in the shade with the ever-present river breeze and a perfect view of the daily chợ trời ritual. With no refrigeration, every family came to the market to purchase their daily food and to visit with friends. When not in school, we often ate at the market—usually a cup of noodle soup while we caught up with friends and exchanged our news of the day.

The items available in the chợ trời varied. Most days, shoppers browsed over fresh-off-the-tree mangos and coconuts, and many varieties of bananas in the fruit section. The distinct aroma of durian fruit found us long before we saw it. The odor of the prickly fruit could be described as turpentine, rotting onions, skunk, and sweaty socks all mixed together. For this reason, many bus drivers refused to allow people to bring it onboard. Whole buildings have called for evacuation because of one forgotten fruit left behind that caused a "possible gas leak" panic.

Despite the stench on the outside, on the inside, durian fruit is a combination of sweet and savory custard. If you can imagine onions and garlic mixed with sugary caramel stirred into whipped cream, you might be close to imagining the flavor. I parked myself near that vendor for the sheer entertainment of watching people nearly gag when they sniffed it for the first time, followed by their animated expressions when offered a bite. An acquired taste, I suppose.

Another section of the chợ trời housed all sorts of leafy greens, colorful potatoes and a variety of luscious fresh vegetables. We sorted through, found the freshest and most vibrantly colored assortment, and gathered plenty of those for our meals each day.

The meat section included live animals, some roped to their vendor, that filled the air with bleats and clucks, and the stench of their assorted droppings. Some swam in tanks, and still other larger animals were already slaughtered and hanging.

A plentiful assortment of river eels squirmed in tanks to be sold by weight. We carried them home in plastic bags with a little water. Once home, we stood guard to retrieve any runaways until Mẹ could administer a mallet to their head that ended their escape attempts. Occasionally a fugitive beat the odds and escaped down the drain. A boiling water bath and thorough scraping removed their slimy coating. Then they were gutted and sliced into four-inch pieces, and cooked with lemongrass and turmeric. Served over white rice, river eels made a tasty meal.

Vendors in different booths offered freshly caught fish dangling from lines or live in tanks. The aroma of the ever-popular crispy dried fish saturated our entire riverside community. A staple at our house, larger dried fish made a scrumptious meal when seared over the grill, pulled from the bone, then served over rice. Add my mom's egg rolls and we had the perfect meal. Adding Mẹ's egg rolls to any meal made it perfect.

We liked fish any way it could possibly be prepared and never wasted any part. Once gutted, we would grill or fry them, bones, head, eyes, fins, and all. Then we picked out the tender meat and ate around the bones. Boiled fish bones and heads made great stock for soup.

Most vendors with dried fish displayed them stacked and sorted by type and size. They mounded gallons of beautiful dried shrimp in huge bowls by size. While a man fished in the river, his wife sat under the shade of her coolie hat and fished for customers at their "store." Surrounded by the bowls, this vendor lured customers with a continual vocal advertisement of the supreme quality of her shrimp to those near and far—no megaphone needed. When a customer glanced in her direction they heard even more of the shrimps' superior quality and flavor. She eventually reeled them in and weighed out the amount of pink delight they needed, then wrapped it up for them.

Some days, Mẹ found a nice piece of hanging meat from a butchered cow, lamb, or pig, and placed her order for a certain number of grams of the meat. One of us came back later after we finished shopping and visiting, picked it up—already sliced, weighed, and wrapped.

When my mother bought a live chicken, I retrieved it about twenty minutes later, butchered and wrapped—feathers, feet and all. Once home, my job began. We placed the meat in a pail and poured boiling water over it that produced the worst smell in all the market, including the durian fruit.

After the water and chicken cooled enough to handle, I plucked feathers. The big feathers came out much easier than the smaller ones that hid underneath. They required tweezers and time. We frugally used every part including organs and feet. Steamed chicken feet are pretty tender. Maybe a little chewy.

On special occasions we enjoyed the delicacy of balut, duck eggs. These partially developed duck embryos were between two and three weeks developed, though some men proved their masculinity by eating those a little more developed and crunchy.

The eggs boiled in salty water about half an hour before we placed them, pointed end down, into a cup. We tapped the fat end of the shell with a spoon and picked out a hole in it about the size of a coin, careful that no shells fell in. Then we pinched away the membrane and revealed the broth. Stirring salt, pepper and other seasonings into the exposed soupy part, we sucked the juiciness into our mouth directly from the shell. Then we broke away the remaining shell, sprinkled the egg with more seasonings, enjoyed the remaining few bites with a fork, or peeled the whole thing, held it in our hand and ate it one bite at a time.

Though the duck beak, eyes, feet, and legs were clearly formed, the softness of the bones allowed us to eat everything inside the shell. And yes, it tastes somewhat like chicken. Pregnant women ate balut before delivery to give them and their unborn child extra vitamins and strength for the birth.

The aromas of fish drying, livestock and their inevitable droppings, a variety of items cooking in the open, not to mention the durian fruit, all simmered and swirled together into a not-so-appetizing combination. To me, those mismatched smells that floated through the chợ trời represented life, abundance, and family.

~~~

Smells aside, I considered our market an enchanting place, made even more marvelous when Ông Nội gave me money to buy candies or trinkets to sell to the children as their parents shopped in the open-air market. I perched myself on his front-porch steps, targeted children shopping with their mothers in the market and gave them my best sales pitch.

Rewarded with cold hard cash in exchange for the trinkets, I bought more things, sold them and increased my empire. Ông Nội even let me buy sugarcane wholesale to resell to adults, again from the front steps of his home—more on-the-job-training for my career as an important and wealthy merchant, and heir to the family business.

Once, Mẹ heard about some coffee beans available at an unusually good price, but she didn't want to take the time to sell them to the individual cafés in town. Because of my vast experience in selling merchandise, I had an idea, tapped her arm, and shared it with her. "Mẹ, if you loan me enough money to buy the beans, I will take them to all the sandwich shops and bakeries and sell them. I can do it. Would you loan me the money? Please?"

My mom smiled coyly, nodded in agreement about my abilities. She turned toward the cash drawer, reached into a special pocket in her waistband, retrieved the key to the drawer, and pulled out some money for the investment.

I purchased the coffee beans and brought the splendid haul to the local business owners along with the pertinent details of the superior quality of those lovely beans, and the grand profit they could make. How could they resist such an opportunity? I sold every coffee bean and made a profit too. If only school could have been that fun.

Often, I carried our food-for-the-day basket from the market back home to our cook—with instructions for preparation—while my mother lingered at the chợ trời and chatted with friends. Because of our extraordinary wealth, we not only employed a cook, but also a maid and a babysitter. We had someone with us at all times. Kidnappers actively looked for children of wealthy parents and had already snatched one cousin.

After gathering our food for the day and a good lunch, we children settled in for an afternoon nap. Then we enjoyed afternoon snacks, sometimes corn with anchovies.

~~~

Like most homes, Ông Nội's took advantage of any

cool breeze the river offered with open windows and floorplan. We shared meals in traditional style—seated on the wooden floor. At home we laid a cloth on the floor and placed serving bowls of food directly on it. At Ông Nội's house they used a low table for the food bowls. Either way, a large bowl of perfectly cooked white rice always held the center spot.

Smaller bowls of vegetables, fish, pork or beef surrounded the rice bowl. We each used fist-sized bowls for our individual meals and filled them at least half-full with rice, then added some vegetables, finally topping it with a little meat. Ông Nội made careful notice of anyone who let their elbows touch the table and corrected the situation with a searing look.

Although one of the wealthiest people in the province, my ông nội remained generous to family and his neighbors. He even funded a hospital that bore his name, and of course, always gave his grandchildren a little spending money of their own. Always looking for ways to share something extra special with us—usually food—he often splurged on an exceptional fish he spotted in the chợ trời. His motto: "we can wear rags but we can have the best food." So, because of his love for us, he lavished us with the best food he could find. That special joy we shared together as a family far outweighed having more "things."

Of all my grandparents, Ông Nội's kindness and gentleness probably influenced me the most. After the last customers made their purchases from all his businesses, someone carted home the money in a small wheelbarrow-type buggy. Once home and dumped out onto the floor, my job began. My eight-year-old hands sorted, smoothed, and flattened out the wadded-up currency. It was my contribution to the family business and good practice for my future as a wealthy entrepreneur.

Once, those young entrepreneur hands secretly tucked a few of those bills into my waistband. When I finished my smoothing job and stood up, my secrets fell out. I felt small enough to have slipped through a crack in the wooden floor—and wished I could. My humiliation rushed to my face and pounded at my temples when everyone stopped to look at me. I held my breath for the consequences.

My father's father didn't yell at me. He didn't stand over me to chastise me, he didn't make a big deal about it in front of the rest of the family at all. My grandfather tenderly reached out to touch my chin and raised it level with his. Locking eyes with me, he simply said, "If you wanted something, all you had to do was ask."

A beating would have hurt less. Everyone took their cue from him, refocused on the job at hand while I slunk away in my shame.

~~~

Our family businesses flourished. At one time, we used a building adjacent to our home for a Fanta soft drink-bottling company. We stored extra bags of flour in our spacious home to give the nearby bakery much-needed storefront space for cooking and selling.

We even sold ice from our home. Although most people couldn't afford a freezer or the electricity to use one, we owned one and used it to make ice in quart-sized cylinders. Customers came to our home for their ice of the day. The freezer had sufficient space to hold one frozen cylinder and have another one freezing. So, we repeated the process as each one sold.

Our freezer had only one job—produce income from the ice, not store leftover food. We cooked what we needed for each meal. Those in our community who did not have such wealth knew if they came to our doorway at night, we might have leftovers from our meal. We quietly shared them with any hungry family.

While most people had some sort of transportation, a bicycle or a motorcycle, we owned more than one motorcycle and owned a car. We had everything anyone could ever want, at least in a small riverside town. I could have anything I wanted, and truly enjoyed my "spoiled little rich girl" life.

~~~

Because in Vietnamese culture, family and respect are of utmost value, we spoke to and about our elders with great respect. Young family members called older family members according to their position in the family rather than use their given names. Even though my aunt arrived as the fifth daughter, according to Vietnamese tradition, I called my aunt who lived in Saigon, Cô Sáu, literally "aunt six."

Spending time with family members who lived out of town brought great adventures to my summer vacations. My adventures in Saigon with Cô Sáu were exceptionally exciting for me. The modern homes in that metropolitan area were unlike our casual open homes in Tân Châu. Those sported crisp clean lines with a formal style.

My aunt sometimes took me to the nearby beach. The Mekong always held a special place in my heart, but this stunning beach had sparkling soft-on-the-feet sand and nonstop salt water waves crashing onto the shore. From indoor swimming pools to stores that sold modern stylish clothes and shoes, I took it all in and relished every minute of our grand adventures.

Once, Cô Sáu bought me a wonderful leather satchel with a buckle closure. The fine smooth leather smelled of the extravagant city. It instantly became my prized possession and stayed tucked securely under my arm for all to see and envy. My hands often wandered over every curve and fold of the glove-soft leather. Because I gave such little attention to my school work, my family teased me mercilessly when I carried my "scholarly" satchel.

Our summertime exploration of this fascinating city made me yearn for even more adventures in other parts of the world. As much as I loved life in Tân Châu, I also enjoyed this different type of life with excitement, adventure, activities and people. My friends daydreamed of marrying someone in their school or their city. I didn't. I longed for extraordinary adventures outside the borders of Vietnam, which never included a vision of marriage to a Vietnamese man.

~~~

I also looked forward to another summer ritual, spending time with my maternal grandparents. They led quiet lives in a small town in the countryside—at least until the grandchildren came to visit. There, I spent the most carefree days of my life.

Because they lived away from the bigger cities, my grandparents allowed me to roam freely with my siblings and cousins without much supervision or need for protection from kidnappers. We played with yo-yos, climbed palm trees, roved barefoot, caught crawdads by hand in the streams, sloshed through the rice paddies, snacked on wildflowers, picked wild herbs and vegetables, and generally wandered as freely as their chickens, until we were exhausted. At dusk, we used our last ounce of youthful vigor to brush off the leeches and head inside for a meal.

In contrast to the sleek homes in the city, these grandparents lived in a rustic thatch-roofed home. The front door welcomed family and friends to a packed-dirt floor. The land at the back of their home sloped downward toward a riverbank.

To compensate for the unlevel ground, the back walls rested on stilts that brought them to the same height as walls in the front. The dirt floor in the front transitioned to above-ground wide, wooden-plank flooring in the back. They left the back of their home that faced the river open and unobstructed to pull in every cool breeze that drifted over the surface of the water. No electricity needed for nature's perpetual fan.

The raised flooring in the back of their home provided the perfect place for an underground bomb shelter and they cut out a little door in the floor to access it. When the sirens blasted, my grandmother immediately gathered us up in her arms and shuttled us down to the shelter. We huddled there together until the threat passed, then she took us back to bed.

My grandfather spent most days either producing or delivering his personal label of fish sauce, a staple in Vietnamese kitchens and restaurants. His manufacturing process began with whole anchovies he personally selected and layered into large barrels. He spread a heavy layer of salt over the top of that layer, then alternated fish and salt until the barrel reached capacity. He sealed the barrels and allowed the mixture time to ferment anywhere from a few weeks to a few months. At the point of perfect fermentation, he drained the rich liquid, bottled it, sold it to local vendors, then refilled the barrel and started the process again.

The smell of a single anchovy would fill a room. The smell of many barrels full of fermenting anchovies required a separate building downwind from their home. The strategy to have the river breeze come into their home from the back and out the front—brilliant.

When he delivered to restaurants and vendors in my hometown, he always stopped, visited us, and brought the bottled deliciousness with him. He left us some of his fabulous fish sauce, and even some spending money for his grandchildren.

Because of the superb quality of his fish sauce, his business thrived and provided his family a substantial income. He bought luxuries most families in the neighborhood couldn't afford, including a television. At night, he opened his front door and turned up the volume, so the neighbors who would otherwise never have enjoyed such indulgence, could see and hear his television. Neighbors lined up in front of the house, on the street, and even up in the branches of their mango tree every night and watched. Their poor tree couldn't withstand the strain and crumbled under the weight of the audience.

My grandfather's generosity also extended to those who needed to feed their families. He discreetly allowed his neighbors to borrow a bushel of rice, with the simple understanding they would replace it when they could. No interest. No legal contracts. A man-to-man agreement. He survived an abusive childhood after his parents died and moved in with relatives, so he understood hard times. This humble man earned great respect among all who knew him.

His wife, my quiet and gentle grandmother, Ba Ngoai, allowed us to get dirty and be free-roaming children. Every morning Ba Ngoai tied her signature red-and-white checkered scarf over her head, leaving only a little bun of hair peeping out near the base of her neck. She graciously cooked the crawdads we brought home and served them and red rice with no concern for where our elbows landed. Wealthier city families served white rice, which had a cleaner flavor. But our simple meals of red rice, fish, vegetables, and soup eaten while sitting on the wood planks of my grandparents' home were grand enough for any king.

We grandkids did get into a little trouble now and then. Just a little. When we grew bored playing in as much dirt and mud as possible, we searched for new challenges in the neighborhood. Our idle hands developed contests to determine who could sneak into neighbors' yards, climb their guava trees, and pick the fruit without getting caught. We also found rocks and tossed them onto any metal rooftops. Fun for the children, not for the residents.

That poor neighborhood. We were loud but pretty harmless. Even the chickens learned to keep their distance from us rowdy kids. But we savored our summer visits with our country grandparents who let us play to our hearts' delight.

Chapter 3

In our history books, we learned Vietnam had been a French colony since the nineteenth century until Japan invaded our country during the Second World War. Then Ho Chi Minh, a Chinese/Socialist/Communist, established a league—Viet Minh—to free Vietnam from both the French and the Japanese. At the end of World War II, Japan withdrew its forces from Vietnam and left French-educated Emperor Bảo Đại as ruler. Ho Chi Minh and his "Viet Minh freedom forces," took the northern city of Hanoi, declared it a Democratic Republic of Vietnam (DRV), and himself as president.

The conflict between northern and southern Vietnam continued until a decisive battle in May 1954 ended with victory for Ho Chi Minh's northern Viet Minh forces. The French loss at the battle ended almost a century of French colonial rule in the area. That led to a Geneva Conference decision to split Vietnam with Ho Chi Minh in control of North Vietnam, and Bảo Đại in control over us in the south. Then, another strongly anti-Communist politician, Ngo Dinh Diem, pushed Bảo aside and became President of the Republic of Vietnam (GVN), South Vietnam.

Although North and South Vietnam were divided and at odds with each other, the bombs usually kept their distance away from our little town. Most active fighting took place a thousand kilometers away on the other side of the country near the demilitarized zone that divided the north and south. When fighting drifted close to us, we usually had enough warning time to run to the trenches for safety before the bombs reached us.

Ba secretly found a *Voice of America* radio station and listened to the news from an outside perspective, but nothing compared to the first-hand stories we heard at the market. There we learned bits of information about the severe conditions in North Vietnam. People who had friends and family from the Communist region spoke carefully and discreetly about how their friends barely survived by hiding in caves, living outdoors in the canopies of trees, and withering away while trying to live off roots, berries and insects. None of us wanted to believe it could happen to us too, but the fear of it still niggled at us.

With Communism breathing down our backs, everyone was under suspicion. The GVN banned anyone from traveling outside their community with the hope that would stop any spread of propaganda, or at least help them identify those who might promote the Communist agenda.

Because Ba needed to travel to keep our businesses going, he applied for a military ID badge that would grant him permission to go to different cities. In order to secure such a great privilege, he paid an application fee and stayed on the military base while they processed the paperwork and completed a thorough investigation of him.

When Mẹ and I were allowed to visit Ba inside the base, they instructed us to wait in an area with tables and benches until soldiers escorted my father from another area to sit with us. My heart sank to see him dressed in a military uniform and escorted by armed guards. How could they treat him like a common criminal when he only wanted to provide for his family?

The back of my neck bristled, my fists readied, and I drew in a good breath, ready to scream at them. People in the neighborhood already called me "the enforcer." Even at the age of nine, I gave every bully in the neighborhood reason to think before they acted.

Soldiers glared and tilted their rifles toward me, as if they read my thoughts. I lowered my head slightly, hid my wrinkled forehead, and convinced my mouth not to pick a fight or arouse suspicions with armed soldiers. My feet punched the dirt below our bench, but I pretended it was accidental.

This time.

The hair on the back of my neck settled when Ba slid onto the bench across the table from us. While he and Mẹ talked about what she could possibly do to make money for food, the armed soldiers scowled at every move we made and positioned themselves to aim their weapons. My anger restrained by reason more than fear, I clenched my teeth and sat rigid while my heart sprinted. Every muscle so trigger-ready, my head throbbed.

If I caught their attention with any gesture or question, they might think Ba secretly supported the Communists, and kill us all. Hidden below the tabletop, my restless fingers found the hem of my shirt and pulled and twisted it while I wished as hard as I could Ba could leave this place and come home with us.

My wish did not happen that day. The time came for us to leave, but Ba had to stay. He gazed at me and calmly reminded me to take care of my siblings. As the oldest, I had great responsibility.

Of course I would. Not many years before, flames from a nearby home threatened the whole neighborhood. My parents got us out of the house, then frantically packed valuables to save.

While they rushed in and out of the house, I waved down a pedicab and loaded my sisters into it. With my most grown-up five-year-old face, I ordered the driver to take them to my aunt's house and pointed to the general area where she lived. I looked him in the eye and told him without hesitation she would pay the fare when he delivered the children, and sent him on his way. "The enforcer" took action when needed, when fire or bullies attacked my family.

I did it before. I would do it again. Releasing my wrinkled hem, I gave Ba my bravest smile, peered into his solemn eyes, nodded, and promised him I would. He could always count on me. I would do anything for my family.

My courageous pledge drained every last ounce of bravery from within me. I tried to uncover another portion of valor somewhere inside me, but when we rose from the table, I couldn't find a single drop of it. When we left my father there at the mercy of the

38

glaring soldiers, my heart hurt so much I thought it would explode in my chest.

I tucked my lips between my teeth to hold back my outward emotions. Face lowered, I held my breath, and plodded alongside Mẹ with strong deliberate steps, kicking the dirt again—just to hit something.

When Ba and the soldiers could no longer see me, I exhaled, released a flood of tears, and sobbed uncontrollably. How could they suspect Ba of anything? What would they do to him? How long would we be separated? What would happen to us? Were we going to become like the North Vietnamese and starve?

My mother consoled me, but my broken heart only felt the emptiness of leaving Ba behind and returning to a fatherless home. Nothing either of us could say or do, absolutely nothing, could change that. The giant mantle of helplessness weighed heavily on my pint-sized shoulders.

If Ba could obtain that travel ID badge and keep the businesses going, and the GVN could keep out the Communists, we would survive. But we also had to gather enough food to live for week after week, until they decided to give him the travel ID badge. We learned during that month that with enough water and fish sauce, a little rice went a long way toward feeding six children.

~~~

Meanwhile, the Cold War escalated with the United States and Soviet Union taking opposite positions in many areas, including our divided Vietnam. The United States backed the South Vietnamese and our quest for a free Capitalistic lifestyle. Soviet Union and China backed the Communist agenda. War continued.

Decades of war took the lives of two million Vietnamese and wounded another three million. More explosives rained down on Vietnam than the allies used on Germany and Japan together in the Second World War[i]. That didn't even include hundreds of tons of napalm jelly[ii], which stuck to its victims while it roasted their skin; white phosphorous, which burned down to the bone; fragmentation bombs, which hurled ball bearings and steel shards in all directions; and toxic chemicals, including Agent Orange, which killed vegetation and inflicted illness on those who were exposed to it.

Despite the 1973 signing of the Paris Peace Accord, peace did not find us. The United States withdrew their military involvement of South Vietnam in August of that year, with the hope the local military could fight their own battle. They could not.

With little manpower to resist them, the Communists overtook one village after another. Explosions drifted closer, then came to our town, and killed people I knew. The fate of the snack-maker family became more and more common. Our land, our people, all became drenched under the tidal wave of war.

~~~

In April 1975, we could not hold out against the invading North. Our South Vietnamese President General Dương Van Minh announced the surrender "to avoid more bloodshed."[iii] The war between the two Vietnams ended with the fall of our lovely Saigon. The Communist North Vietnamese government promptly renamed it Ho Chi Minh City. With one statement,

North and South Vietnam once again became united under a hardline Communist government—our Capitalistic government completely dissolved, and we owned nothing.

The day after Saigon fell, soldiers paraded—brooms in hand—down our street, in front of our home. Their dark green uniforms and helmets with a red star announced their Communist affiliation. How exciting. Soldiers in our little town marching right in front of us and sweeping our streets.

My excitement faded as I realized their scrawny bodies validated the truth we heard in the market about life in North Vietnam. They symbolically swept away the dust and dirt of yesterday's freedom and announced the new Communist regime among us. They proudly nodded and flexed their muscles to impress us with their power as they strutted along the street. I turned my face away from them to hide my smirk when I realized their brilliance must be hidden behind the feminine napkins they found and strapped over their noses and mouths while they finished their dusty job.

I glanced at my parents, who did not share my excitement or humor for even a moment. They wore masks of calm on their faces, but their stiffened stance told me something unsettled them about the scene. Questions would have to wait until we could speak in private.

Before that day, we suspected certain people worked as spies for the Communists. The day the soldiers declared their presence, those we thought might be acting as spies suddenly received positions of leadership within the city. Their reward for faithfulness to the Party confirmed our suspicions. As the transition of power took place, the community settled into the new reality that the government owned everything around us, and every aspect of our lives. With no one on our side anymore, we had no option but to submit. Our worst fears came to pass.

They installed loudspeakers in our town and blasted wake-up music through them every morning. The speakers shouted out basic news, Communist-themed music, along with a pep talk about the wonderful "life of equality under Communism." With no way to shield ourselves from the speakers, we simply endured daily lectures and mentally tuned out the propaganda.

~~~

Pol Pot came into power over our northern neighbor, Cambodia. He spent years in France studying Stalin, Marx, Mao, and Lenin and while there, he joined the Communist Party. When he returned to Cambodia, he joined the Marxist-Leninist Khmer Viet Minh organization set up by Ho Chi Minh. According to Pot's own words, he planned to "create a classless society," and "exterminate the fifty-million Vietnamese and purify the masses of the [Cambodian] people."[iv]

Cambodia's Prime Minister, Long Boret, wanted to negotiate some peaceful resolution with Pot. The US Ambassador to Cambodia, John Gunther Dean, reported Prime Minister Boret "stayed in Cambodia, thinking that he could have some kind of dialogue with the Khmer Rouge. When he realized that was impossible, he raced to the airport with his family in a jeep to try and get out of the country. When they arrived at the airport, they got on a helicopter with some military officers. One officer brutally shoved him off the helicopter. The copter took off. The Khmer Rouge captured Long Boret and his family and killed them all."[v]

Pot made it clear he would neither negotiate nor tolerate any resistance. He outlawed books and religion[vi], set up collective farms, and assigned people to hard labor there. Reluctance to submit to the assignment brought certain death, after suitable torture. The mass killings, starvation and disease under his direction and policies brought death to millions.[vii]

These "killing fields" could not hold all the dead, so Pol Pot dumped them into my once sparkling, vibrant, life-giving Mekong River. Instead of transporting items for trade and providing abundant fish, the Mekong now transported the decomposing bodies of the massacred from Cambodia to their final resting place in the South China Sea. Unhindered, Pot's Khmer Rouge "cleansing" continued. Now filled with death, my parents forbade me to go near my marvelous Mekong.

Curiosity and habit drew me to the heart of our little town, despite my parents' warning. I had to go look. My heart sickened as I watched lifeless bodies and body parts—sometimes only a head—bob up and down in the channel of the waterway. Once filled with life and trade, my beautiful river now swirled with rotting human flesh. The stench drifted up the bank and met me with a cruel slap. I covered my mouth and nose so I could fully take in the scene. Devastated and mesmerized at the same time, I came back day after day to see if perhaps it were only a bad dream. The nightmare continued for long months, maybe even a year.

I dragged my siblings by the arm to come and see the sight. We watched as people covered their faces, gathered near the river edge, and kicked stray bodies and limbs back into the channel. The results of Pot's Khmer Rouge cleansing operation in Cambodia now defiled our river, our town, and our lungs.

The air no longer carried delightful chatter among the boat merchants along the Mekong behind Ông Nội's house. Even the laughter and squeals from playing children across the river vanished—replaced with thick silence and despair.

Blood-curdling screams pierced the stillness when daily Khmer Rouge patrols inflicted their torment. I listened and watched helplessly from my side of the Mekong, while the Khmer Rouge randomly chose another family for the torture of the day. The pitiful cries and pleas never brought about any mercy. Only when the soldiers tired of their brutal games did the affliction end.

They punctuated their mission by setting fire to the home. My stomach churned for these families, yet my eyes could not pull away. No longer just stories in the market or an occasional bomb. Now, these cold-blooded killers performed their unspeakable carnage right across the river from us.

Pot's determination didn't stop at the Cambodian side of the Mekong. The familiar high-pitched scream of a bomb descending ended in my beloved market, filled with my friends, relatives, and neighbors. Its deafening explosion brought the same whoosh of dirt and smoke, followed by a rain of rubble, and fires, and death, as that day at school.

My hearing again muffled into silence despite the

explosions I could see before me. My eyes burned. My throat thickened with acrid smoke and the taste of metal. Time again crept in slow motion while the dust settled. I couldn't bear looking, yet I had to know. I shielded my mouth and watched as the outcome revealed itself.

A circle of devastation lay before me. On the outer perimeter nearest to me, my injured friends and neighbors assessed their injuries, brushed off the dust, and pulled themselves up from the ground. A little beyond me, horrible wretched cries of those burning alive rang in chorus with mothers who screamed out for their children. Beyond them were twisted but intact friends. Even closer to the center of the devastation, detached human limbs mingled with those of the livestock brought to the market. In the middle, only flaming shell fragments remained.

Dust-covered children cried out for their parents. Brothers and sisters clung to lifeless bodies that would never play with them again. Fires raged without pity. The lifeblood of so many spilled, splattered, and stained our little community again.

I watched the dying finish their cries. The bloodied survivors leaned on each other to help find their living and gather their dead.

My "spoiled little rich girl" days sank beneath the somber, heavy days that now filled our reality. Our family, our town, our lives, all shared in the intense suffering of the war.

The dust settled.

Time ticked in its proper rhythm again.

The wheelbarrows that normally carried produce in and out of the market now ushered the dead away from the market one last time.

My ears and eyes now forever were tainted with another scene that would never be washed away. Clearly, our lives in Vietnam would never be the same.

~~~

The new Socialist government took over production companies and banned all private business and land ownership "to equalize the people." They nationalized every business, even the street vendors, stripping us of our means of making a living "in order to give to the poor." Even the banks and the money within them now belonged to the government. Our pockets emptied and their pockets filled.

My great-grandfather sacrificed and worked hard building up businesses that supported his family for generations, just to have this new government steal it from him.

From us all.

With no hope of ever retrieving any of it, and no way to fight the process, my precious great-grandfather's heart couldn't take the strain of the loss. We lit incense as we mourned for him, our livelihood, our freedom, and the world as we knew it.

Realizing our currency would become completely worthless, my mother quietly purchased non-perishables such as large bags of rice with our remaining cash and exchanged the rest for gold ingots. Unlike our decadent lifestyle as a French colony, we no longer bought new clothes, butter, and champagne. We stretched what we used to spend in one day to last many days. Mẹ stopped preparing a bowl of food for herself at mealtime and sat to the side until we finished eating our small portions. Then she discreetly swished her fingertip around the bowl to scoop out any leftover crumbs as her meal.

The new government expected many South Vietnamese people who had some money and/or education to resist this new era of government control and initiate a rebellion. They decided doctors and educators and others employed in such occupations, along with anyone who wore glasses or had books in their homes might have the intellect to "think improperly" and thus posed a "possible threat." So, they ordered nearly half a million people to re-education camps to erase these improper thoughts.

They assigned Dương Mười, a former Naval officer for Southern Vietnam, to undergo "training" at a re-education camp. The sole mission inside that camp: rob these military or outspoken "possible threats" of their individual or collective strength to challenge the regime. They routinely beat, tortured, starved, and forced unreasonably hard labor on their prisoners to complete their "training/education." If that didn't work, execution served as the quick resolution for anyone who exhibited any spark of resistance, ending any hope for them and dimming any glimmer of hope for all those forced to watch. Anything other than complete silent submission resulted in death.

Those who managed to survive returned home as empty shells.

~~~

Communist officials planted themselves in cities and kept an eye on everyone during the transition from our life of freedom and Capitalism, to the new Communist rule. Because we previously owned businesses and money, one official and his family moved in with us.

The official appeared unarmed, but he was obliged to report anything suspicious.

The Fanta bottling business no longer existed, so they moved into that area of our home for a couple of years. There, they'd be aware of all our activities and still have a separate place to cook and eat their own meals. The husband and wife appeared to be in their thirties. They had a daughter the same age as one of my sisters, and three elementary age sons. The mom looked like every other Vietnamese woman in the city. The official's long-sleeved shirts barely disguised his bony frame but signified his important position. Realizing they were poor, my parents shared a little food and conversation with them.

The Communist government now owned all land, businesses, banks and our funds within them. So with these eyes in our home, we exercised extreme diligence in how we spent any remaining money, and how we retrieved money from any "hiding places." We couldn't be seen gathering with others; that would put us under suspicion of planning an uprising or rebellion. Nothing could appear out of the ordinary or anti-government. Even whispering took place far away from them. Neighbors kept their distance and changed their conversations quickly when these "spies" came near. A casual remark about a long line at the post office resulted in public flogging if the wrong person heard about it.

Communism under the guise of Socialism had appealed to the poor because of their promise of equalization. In fact, they kept that promise, but not how the poor expected. Instead of the poor moving out of poverty, they remained in poverty and the rest of us joined them. The government determined the value of everything. Our crops, our labor, our lives were valued according to our contribution to the government. No supply and demand. Only demand.

They took everything we owned as they tried to take our very souls. Under these desperate conditions, many secretly searched for a way to get out of this sinking country. Surrounded by Communist countries, the South China Sea became the only possible hope for escape.

Chapter 4

L iving in the tropics, our normal temperatures reached into the eighties and nineties during the day and dropped about ten degrees at night. Like the other homes in this steamy climate, our windows had no glass, only some bars to keep out large predators. This open design made use of the shade and encouraged breezes to flow from room to room. Back when we had the wealth to afford such things, electric fans provided all the air conditioning we needed.

The official and his family stayed in their separate wing of the home at night. My parents slept on the first floor, behind the closed and padlocked accordion-metal doors. The six of us children slept on the second-floor all-purpose gathering, eating, bathing, and sleeping room.

Running water from the city system flowed at will from a faucet in this upstairs room into a concrete reservoir that held about a hundred and fifty gallons. Because the water only flowed for short periods, usually at night but we never knew when, we simply left the faucet valve open. It never offered us enough at any one time to overflow.

Each morning, we emptied some water from the reservoir into a basin, then used the water in that basin for cleaning and cooking for the day. We poured some into an upright cannister-type filter for drinking. At the end of the day or anytime we needed to clean our hands or faces, we dipped washcloths into the basin and used that to wipe off the sweat and grime.

After we ate our evening meal, we children went outside and played hopscotch, jumped rope, or tossed a ball until dark. When the mosquitoes came out, we went in to try to avoid the ever-present danger of mosquito-borne diseases such as Dengue Fever. We used our washcloths for our evening wipe-down baths before we slept.

One evening, Cô Sau visited us before dark and spoke with my parents in hushed tones outside the hearing of our resident official. While they whispered, we children went upstairs to prepare for bedtime. After cleaning up, we pitched a mosquito-net tent to discourage disease-carrying insects from eating us alive while we slept. We slid out the neatly folded netting from its daytime spot in a trunk and carefully unfolded it. Then our fingers found the loops around its top edge and hooked those loops over nails positioned around the ceiling, creating a room-size sleep canopy over our all-purpose dining and bedroom floor.

Normally, all six children gathered and slept under the netting. That May evening two sisters, Thu and Xinh, had already started their summer visits with out-of-town relatives, leaving four siblings to stretch out on the smooth cool floor.

The net kept out most of the flying insects, but families of mice—including all their cousins and neighbors—easily nudged under the netting and found their way to any crumbs or spills from our latest meal. They sniffed around in circles for any leftover morsels without hurting us, so we gently brushed the little rodents aside when their whiskers and warm fur tickled us during the night.

Near the edge of the stairs, I heard some of the discussion below. My aunt spoke to my parents about a plan to leave for Australia by boat. "Remember Ông Phồn Tam who owns the boat? We have done business with him before. He plans to leave by boat from Bac Liêu on the southern coast and go to Australia, and will take as many as he can with him. A family who registered to leave as refugees and planned to leave with him backed out. Cô Muoi's family fits their description and they are going to take the place of that family. There might be room for you all, or at least some of your children—if you have the money."

"How much?" Ba inquired.

"Six ounces of gold. Per person."

Ba reminded her, "We have not registered to leave under refugee status. If they catch us—"

Cô Sau interrupted, "We have nothing left here. The longer we wait, the worse it is going to be. We are taking this chance to try to get out."

I could hardly believe Cô Muoi and Cô Sáu and their families were leaving. Most adult conversations revolved around the idea that the best—maybe the only—means of survival required escaping Vietnam. Now my family considered our dwindling options.

Over the last months, private whispers multiplied in the market of relatives who died when their overloaded boats sank. Still others received word their family members were seized by Thai pirates who murdered the men and sold the girls into slavery. Now and then someone made it safely to Australia. A couple of our cousins lived there, but survival stories were rare.

I strained to hear more of their conversation. She reminded them about the urgency to leave with monsoon season due to begin any day and Communism gaining more authority all the time. How much longer would officials agree to look aside with gold persuasion? They had accepted the "legal" bribe to turn their heads if their family left tonight, with no guarantee of what might happen tomorrow. This could be the chance, perhaps the last chance, to escape. "You should come—if you can afford it. If you can only send some of the children, I will help look after them, but Ông Tam will leave soon. You have to decide tonight whether you want to get on his boat. We are heading to Bac Liêu early in the morning."

"It's a lot to think about. We will consider it," Ba told her.

After Cô Sau left, Ba padlocked the front doors behind her with agonizing decisions to make.

"We don't have time to go get Thu and Xinh and bring them back, much less register," Ba started.

"You're right. If we were caught without registration or raised any suspicions by getting them early—" Mẹ agreed.

Ba said, "On the other hand, how can we turn down the opportunity to give our children a chance to live in freedom?"

Mẹ responded, "Or we could all stay together. Would it be better for them to die in the sea than to die in our home?"

Ba agreed. "How could we possibly separate? How could we send them to their deaths or to a life of slavery? We have always faced everything together."

Silence.

The quiet allowed me a moment to think. Already stripped of most of their wealth, would there be enough hidden money to get us all out? My head swirled with possibilities. We barely bought essentials. We had no extra money for bribes. As a family with six children, what would my parents do?

Most people made the equivalent of a two, maybe three, ounces of gold per year. This trip required six ounces.

Six ounces per person.

Ba broke the silence. "We have enough gold to get one out. We can at least give one child a chance to escape this."

My mother replied, "Two. We have enough to send two."

She had hidden money even Ba didn't know about. My parents moved away from my hearing and my ears only caught the familiar sounds of their normal evening routine as they pulled out their bedding from the chest in the front room.

Aware their whispered conversations continued below me but no longer within my hearing, I joined Loan, Duyên, and Tham under the netting on the wide wooden boards where we enjoyed so many meals, giggles, and dreams. A real possibility existed we might leave this place forever tonight. I placed a pretend smile on my face so my younger siblings wouldn't suspect anything. If they cried or spoke out loud, the plan might be exposed, and I couldn't risk that.

The evening breeze outside our window brought in a goodnight kiss of fresh night air. I tossed my hair back over my shoulder, turned my head toward the window to get the full breeze across my face, and scanned the room that held so many memories. Above the barred window, pictures of my parents watched over us. The wooden bench in front of the window provided me a place to contemplate my little-girl thoughts while I gazed out over the patio. That's where our maid used to hang our clothes out to dry, but the days of hiring cooks, nannies, and maids were gone.

The unused fan gathered dust. We had no money for such a luxurious use of electricity now. Back when we could afford extravagant things such as having pictures taken, I stood beside the fan for a portrait, a not-so-subtle picture of our wealth.

The locked glass cabinet still held our family treasures—a clock, some delicate crystal figurines, and a bottle of perfume reserved for New Year's celebrations. I closed my eyes and remembered the tender touch of my mother dabbing a drop on my wrist, and the sweet scent it brought for our new year.

The armoire that held our clothes stood tall and unphased by our predicament. Inside its closed double doors, our matching floral, light-weight pajama-like clothes hung clean and ready for the next day. Because we could now only afford one bolt of fabric to make clothes for all six of us, even our little brother sported the same floral design his five sisters wore. Each day we dressed, then made our final inspection from the armoire's full-length mirrored door before we headed out for the day. Would it ever hold my face in its reflection again? Would our new home in Australia have such things?

My morning routine might never again include gathering water from the concrete cistern. If we did leave that night, it would stay behind and keep the secret of my scorched fingers safe with it.

I held my pretend smile in place, turned my head to the side, and wiped stray tears. I pulled my little brother close to me, a precious toddler I often carried on my hip as I stroked his cool black hair into place. As he nodded off to sleep, I snuggled with him and memorized the feel and smell of home and family.

If they sent me away to Australia, would I ever see any of my family after tonight? If I left and could return, would they be here? Could they survive? If the officials reported this kind of treason what would happen to Ba?

No, I couldn't think about those things now. I had to set my mind toward the journey ahead. It probably held a wonderful adventure filled with new people, new landscapes, new foods, even my non-Vietnamese husband, and I would be able to share the new adventure with my family as soon as we settled in.

Long before the sun came into my window, my parents came upstairs and whispered that the two oldest children, my sister Loan and I, were going on a trip, but we were not to speak of it with anyone. They said it would be for the best. Loan and I obediently pulled back the netting and slipped out without waking the other two.

They concocted a cover story that my sister and I were going to visit our grandparents to try to hide our scheme from any curious observers. They already gathered a small bag of rice and dried fish to sustain us a few days, along with a change of clothes.

My mother placed all my bracelets and necklaces of value on me, to be sold as needed when we reached Australia. She instructed me to stuff the jewelry into my mouth for safekeeping, should anyone try to take it. She and I both knew she meant pirates, and if pirates attacked we wouldn't likely survive. At least it gave me and my sister some hope. If we needed anything for this trip, we needed hope.

We tiptoed down the steps long before the early-morning radio loudspeaker blasted out the daily propaganda of how wonderful and trustworthy Communists were to their adoring public.

We passed the Dương family home sign and padded toward the front door. We left the two witnesses to our escape sitting cross-legged and silent, waiting for incense and prayers. My cone-shaped coolie hat remained stacked with the others by the door. I wouldn't need it in Australia.

My father stopped inside the door and listened for any activity other than the crickets. We froze in place behind him, barely breathing. He inserted the key into the padlock on our front doors, turned it, pulled gently, and released the lock with only a slight click. Without making another sound, he lifted it from the latch and eased one door to the side.

He peeped out and listened again.

With nothing moving except the mosquitoes, the three of us slipped out of our Tân Châu home without disturbing the birds nesting in the guava tree. If they woke, their squawks would alert the whole neighborhood. The birds were in their place, but didn't raise their heads.

Ba handed the padlock key to my mother who pulled back inside and gently closed the doors behind us. I heard a faint snap, no louder than the chirps of the crickets, when she replaced the lock.

We joined my other family members and boarded a public transportation bus headed to the south coast. The drive on rough dirt roads to the southern coastal city of Bac Liêu took several hours. Our bus bounded over the rough roads, and we bounced and swayed in unison. All passengers' eyes were the same, downcast, weary, and troubled. A strange quiet surrounded us instead of the normal friendly chitchat among passengers or families. We carried the same burdens and dreams, and fear of what would happen if we spoke them out loud.

The time for tears or emotion had already passed. Calm and quietness prevailed over us as the resolve for the mission ahead became our sole focus. We settled into the rhythm of the tires on the road. Out the window, I watched the familiar rivers, streams, and rice paddies pass by while the mountains shrank behind us.

Though my mind raced ahead with possibilities of life in Australia, the bus meandered slowly and deliberately around potholes on the rough roads. I eagerly anticipated this great adventure of traveling to a new land and tried to mentally prepare for the wonderful new life south of the equator.

~~~

We arrived at Bạc Liêu and found Cô Sau and her husband, along with another aunt and her husband and their two boys, and another uncle. We gathered in a huddle and the adults reviewed the plan.

I stood with them and took in the scene on the boat dock in front of me. Most of my life revolved around boat docks. The air always held the smell of fish and the sound of laughter from the fishermen who compared their catches of the day. Never had I witnessed a scene like this. Fog hovered over the boats and the docks around them. As the fog shifted in and out, I glimpsed families wandering around and heard a chorus of weeping.

We joined the crowd who shuffled along the wooden dock. The thickness of the mist allowed us to see only a short distance at a time. As though we passed through rooms, we could see only one boat at a time, and the scene around it. Each room, each boat told the same story. The loudest cries matched those I saw within our "room," but wails of the unseen filled the air.

In this room, a father lifted his screaming toddler high up to waiting hands of strangers aboard a boat, while his face contorted into an anguished grimace. When the screaming child left his hands, it took the very breath from him. He gasped as though unseen hands choked his throat.

My eyes followed him as he backed away, collapsed in a corner, and succumbed to nauseating groans that spoke more than any words could ever express. Other fathers stepped forward—one by one—and delivered their precious cargo. Then each turned away, slouched over, and pressed their empty arms against the pain in their hearts. They trudged heavily into gray corners, slumped onto the dock, while groans erupted from the deepest part of their souls.

We made our way past boat after boat and encountered more despondent, childless parents. One mother stumbled aimlessly away from a boat as her fists pounded against the side of her head in utter disbelief of what they had been compelled to do. Oblivious to us, she repeated out loud the names of children she would likely never see again—yet would never forget—then faded into the mist.

We waded through a parade of misery thicker than the fog. I stayed as close to Ba as I could get without tripping us both.

~~~

My father found his friend, the boat owner, Ông Phồn Tam. After the greetings, he explained the obvious complication to Ba. As the reality of the true state of the country sank in, more and more people wanted to escape. The scene of chaos and desperation on the dock grew more impassioned every day. The number of people who wanted to leave on his boat already far outweighed the capacity of the vessel. Even when he considered pushing the limits of what the little riverboat could possibly manage, he had to draw the line.

After his explanation and sincere apology, the boat owner told my father we might as well turn around and go back home. It would be impossible for us to get on the boat.

We came prepared for the journey and didn't give up easily. Ông Phồn Tam wouldn't leave for another day or two, so we stayed. Just in case. Until he left, we clung to the slim possibility he might change his mind or somehow make room for us. After some time, my uncle, Bac Ba, took the owner's advice, left with his family and returned home to Tân Châu.

When Ba announced we might as well go back home too, I still had one more "spoiled little rich girl" fit left in me and I used it then and there. I would not go back. I begged, "Ba, please let me stay. Ba, please, I do not want to go back. Please, Ba, please, I. Want. To. Stay." I used the foot-stomp, hands-on-hips, big-eye pleading look and every other ploy I could muster. I did not want to miss this adventure. It would be better to lose my life trying to live, than to die without ever trying.

My patient Ba lowered his head. We could wait a while longer. The other aunts and uncles waited with us.

We stayed.

Daylight left.

We waited on the dock anyway, and watched as other riverboats pulled away from shore, packed with so many people they hung over the edge to breathe.

Finally, in the last couple of hours before departing time, Ông Tam pulled my father aside. "I think I can put them on the list," he said.

Before he could change his mind, I filled my lungs with a deep breath of Vietnamese air and took my last bold, fearless steps on the soil of my homeland toward the boat. Armed with rice and dried fish, jewelry, a change of clothes, and a heart filled with expectations of a grand adventure, I strode across the slender wooden plank, carefully placing one foot directly in front of the other until I stepped onto the boat.

I didn't look back to try to find Ba in the darkness. That heartbreaking scene already played out too many times over the last few days with so many other families. I would not contribute to the grief he must already bear. Instead, I focused on strength, composure, and courage for the adventure before me.

That night Ba boarded a bus for the journey back home.

Alone.

My parents shared the wretched dilemma of knowing the bleak odds of either the choice to stay together or the choice to try to get some of us out. They knew the possible outcomes and they knew they would have no easy way to find out our fate. On the outside, they would appear normal, tranquil, no different from any other day. On the inside they would be frantic for news of our safety. Neither parent could share their grief with anyone for fear of giving away our true location and putting the remaining family at risk. Bribes only went so far.

Chapter 5

May 1979

Two weeks after my twelfth birthday

Under cover of darkness, well over four hundred evacuees somehow packed onto little riverboat #MH0010, far exceeding its load capacity. Both the upper and lower decks filled to overflowing with confident and eager evacuees. We squeezed into a spot on the lower deck and sat knees to chest, shoulder to shoulder. With no space to stretch out and lie down, Loan and I leaned on each other. My aunts and uncles and their two sons and my uncle stayed close by, balancing the weight of the world on their shoulders and optimism for a better future in their hearts.

The boat motor hummed to life and managed to push our overloaded vessel into motion. We slipped out from the dock, and the lights of Bạc Liêu shrank in the distance. I took comfort in nestling snugly together as we drifted out farther away from land into the murky shadows of the night sea.

Time would tell how our riverboat held up to the

open sea. Not long after we settled in, my stomach responded poorly to boat travel and it emptied its contents. With every inch of the lower deck filled with people, they shoved me up to the top deck for their own well-being. With some fresh air up top, my stomach adjusted to the waves.

Ocean foam trailed behind us and pointed back to the faint lights of the coast. The bow of the boat parted the gentle sea waves in front of us and created patterns of waves that sparkled with glints of moonlight. What a grand adventure. I inhaled a deep breath of the cool salty air. Ba would be home in a few hours. We would be in Australia in a couple of days. When we were settled, we could send for the whole family. We would be back together soon. It might take a few weeks, maybe a month, but soon.

Certain bribes assured that we slipped out from the port unnoticed. Now we needed to travel far enough out to sea so that a big American ship could see us and take us to Australia.

Some sat. I stood.

We waited, hoped, and wondered what loomed before us in the darkness.

Stars became more visible the farther we motored from the shore. More stars than I had ever seen before sparkled almost close enough to touch. The darkness of the ocean and the sky merged and gave the illusion that our little boat floated along with them.

I had never been so far away from cities.

From land.

From family.

Overwhelming loneliness crept in when I realized how small we were compared to the vastness of the ocean. I blinked hard to keep it from dripping down my cheeks.

We chugged south through the black night.

The sun rose and brought color back to the world. Away from the gray mist of the dock, I saw our little boat in clean sunlight for the first time. Like the rest of us, it suffered from serious neglect, wear and tear, and bore a striking resemblance to a worn-out shoe.

Our eyes continually scanned the horizon for the outline of any big American ship. While we waited for someone to call out a sighting, we chatted among ourselves of the possibilities ahead. We planned our Australian adventures. But we saw no ships, big or American.

We blinked, squinted, and focused our sun-dried eyes against the intense glare of the tropical sun on the water. Still, no ship.

The captain allowed us to use the fresh-water tank and galley in the back of the boat. One of my aunts cooked some of our rice rations. We ate a portion along with some of the dried fish to hold us over until a ship, even if not American, saw us and took us aboard. We needed to save some rations for our arrival Down Under.

The sun rose and set several times, but no ship, big or small, rescued us. Our only companions—the stars and the sharks who stayed nearby.

We'd made it this far. Even without rescuers, we might be able to navigate the sea long enough to make it to Australia on our own. Every passing day the faithful little motor pushed us closer to our goal, and we scanned the horizon for some kindhearted ship to help us reach our destination.

After a few days and nights passed without incident, we encountered a huge Malaysian Navy ship. They claimed we "trespassed" out of international waters into Malaysian waters, but not to worry. The uniformed crewmen informed us they would pull us out to international waters to safety. With no reason for us to protest, the captain allowed them to board our little boat.

But, once aboard, their demeanor changed and they grabbed a young man by the arms, dragged him away from us, and took him by force back to their ship.

My heart dropped.

Their mission had nothing to do with our safety.

They stripped their innocent hostage of his shoes, made sure we all watched, then forced him to stand barefoot on the searing hot metal deck of their ship. His anguish reached us all.

Loudly.

Clearly.

My eyes refused to watch the horrible picture and I lowered my head. The adults around me all sheltered the eyes of their children and pulled them away from that side of the boat. My curious fingers remembered their own painful burns, and I rubbed them in sympathy for the torture his screams described to us. My stomach knotted, helpless to rescue him, and anticipated what they would do to us next.

After agonizing minutes, he became limp and breathless. Before he lapsed into unconsciousness, they pulled him off the scorching metal.

Intimidation accomplished. None of us would take a stand against these barbarians.

The pirates in military uniforms tossed the young

man with piteously charred feet back aboard our boat, gathered metal detectors and guns, and forced their way among us.

We kept our distance from them and held onto our loved ones.

I remembered to stuff my jewelry in between my cheek and teeth. Jaws clenched, eyes down, and fists ready, my heart pounded and my toes curled to hold on to my flip-flops.

Some girls had already planned for this. They dressed like boys and cut their hair in short boy-style cuts. Better to die on the boat than to live—if you call that living—as merchandise in the sex-trading business.

I determined they would not see me cry. They would not.

At first, they focused on the beeps of the detectors and easily located all the gold ingots hidden between the walls of the boat. They gathered them all. Every last one.

Then they strip-searched us but didn't check the secret hiding place of my necklaces, or the diamonds my aunt hid in the chewing gum in her mouth. Some men hid their watches in a barrel of fresh water. The pirates, determined to take everything of value, broke the barrel intending to rob us of our drinking water. When they shattered the barrel and the water spilled out, the hidden treasures were revealed and confiscated.

Meanwhile heavy gray clouds drew closer, rumbling with thunder. The pirates looked up, sized up the storm, and timed out their ability to get back to port before it hit.

Those lazy pirates didn't squander their time or energy on knives, bullets, or taking us to be sold to the highest bidder. Satisfied with the value of their booty and wary of the growing storm, they disabled the motor and radio, poured out our gas, tossed out the maps, then pulled us at high speed out into the open sea. Plenty more refugee boats loaded with treasures would follow this same path. They could come back another day for them. After the storm.

Black clouds swirled in a devilish dance.

Lightening sliced the sky, followed by a continuous percussion of thunder.

They slowed slightly, then released the tow rope. The jolt rocked us. The pirates pointed at us, laughed out loud about their great spoils, and mocked our pending fate. This kind of storm would take care of the rest of their dirty work while they traveled back home, our dreams stashed in their pockets.

Now completely helpless, we floated unnoticed on a toothpick of a boat in the vast South China Sea with a dreadful storm headed directly toward us. The agitated waters twisted us as though we were riding a wild animal. The lightning and booms of thunder blasted across the water like bombs. Torrential rain from above and frothy waves from every side tried to smother us. The briny water slapped our faces and clogged our lungs, stealing our breath with every sudden pounding.

We rode one giant wave after another amid constant lightning. The wind shrieked like evil spirits in our midst, pronouncing a curse on us. We pitched and rolled at the mercy of the sea and wind and held onto anything we could grab. Little MH0010 groaned from the lashing.

The upheaval caused many to cling to the side of the boat for upheavals of their own. Some yelled in frustration and anger. Some wept. Others sat with vacant faces. An older lady climbed to the roof of the boat and cried aloud to God, pleading with Him to spare us, guide us, and preserve us.

I wrapped my arms around my sister as the rain pelted our skin. If we went down, we went down together.

~~~

The frenzy of the storm passed. Passengers stood and assessed the damage to the boat and each other. Loan and I squeezed water out of our hair and pulled our drenched clothes away from our bodies.

Soaked to the bone, but alive.

Our valiant, worn-out shoe of a riverboat weathered a storm like it had never encountered before. Afloat and intact, but so far out in the open sea we could see no land in any direction.

The storm clouds marched on to their next venue, allowing us to see three dark objects on the horizon. When the clouds cleared, the shadowed outline of boats appeared on the horizon. Rescue boats?

Convinced our rescuers only needed to notice our little boat, someone shot up a flare and our hopes with it. Instead of coming toward us, each of the three boats scrambled away from us.

Not rescuers.

More likely, another band of pirates who took the flares as a warning we might be armed, which dismissed their interest.

No land.

No boats.

No way to communicate with any other vessels.

No navigation or power for the boat—not even a

sail.

My parents believed this would be our best hope for survival and the start of a new life. Now it seemed their dreams and mine would never be realized. The boat aimlessly rocked us over gentle waves. We used our dwindling rations of rice and dried fish to flavor the little water we found, and called it "soup." We pretended we had a little life left in us and sipped it.

With nothing but an ocean graveyard in all directions, we stopped chatting about our expectations of life in Australia, much less any long-shot dreams of living in the USA. We sat heads down to avoid the shame of watching life drip out of one another.

Some passengers lit incense and knelt with palms pressed against each other, lifted up to their foreheads. They raised their eyes and searched the skies for a sign that some god smelled the fragrant incense, heard their prayers, and would send help to rescue us.

Others knelt with their foreheads pressed against the floor voicing their pleas to any god. With no breeze, the smoke from their incense circled low among us .

As the clouds thinned, the intense sun dried my hair and clothes, leaving a sticky layer of salty grime. Sea water from the soaked decking transformed into little vapor clouds, then rose up until they disappeared in the sky, taking the few remaining droplets of our dreams with them.

No one spoke. We had no more options to discuss.

Passengers sat with knees to chest on the deck. They lowered their foreheads to rest on their crossed arms and tried to sleep, or perhaps forget their dreams.

Dry again, I tried to think of something encouraging to say to my sister, but she could see the truth as well as I. My heart and mind battled over the dream versus the reality.

Reality won.

My heart lost.

Some slipped into unconsciousness, and death snatched up the weakest. Family members wrapped them in cloths and respectfully lowered them overboard. The captain started a list of their names. Who would be there to bury the last of us?

The ocean waves sloshed up against the sides of our vessel, almost eager to overtake us. I didn't understand why. Empty pockets, bodies, and spirits, we had nothing left to take.

The sun abandoned us for the night and left us alone in a pitch-black darkness that matched our souls.

The mass of stars overhead watched in silence.

The sharks circled with their fins slicing through the waterline. Sometimes they turned to show one eye above the water, waiting for us to join them in the ocean. Only they remained hopeful.

Chapter 6

After weary days without hope, hope appeared on the horizon. Land! Not Australia, but Indonesia. Already overrun with Vietnamese refugees, the Indonesian government didn't have room to bring any more homeless people to the mainland. Instead, a ship pulled our crippled boat near an unestablished island off the main island.

It took time for all of us to jump into the water and wade ashore in our pitiful parade. We struggled to lift our exhausted legs against the shallow waves. Gradually, we trudged our soggy bodies and possessions—mine rolled in my waistband—to the solid sand of our new home.

We stretched our cramped limbs and gathered our bearings. Beyond the shoreline stood tall grass. Past that grassy field, treetops that might be coconut and banana trees waved their fronds to welcome us. Maybe we could at least find some fruit to eat. We wandered into the grass a few yards, but quickly lost sight of one another until we pushed down the stalks.

Both rescued and abandoned at the same time, we had the safety of land, but we had none of the basic resources necessary for life—food, water, and shelter. It appeared we had to find a way to survive on our own.

That night we slept in our gritty clothes on the shoreline, without shelter in the pouring rain. I don't remember ever being so wet for so long. Mẹ always let us play outside in the rain, with the belief that it held special powers of healing. If rainwater did that, we should have been healthy the rest of our lives. When the sun came up, we would look for some sort of shelter and food.

That night, the disappointed sharks had to find a different meal.

~~~

Indonesians from the main island arrived by boat the next day with items to sell. My jewelry would be of no benefit to us if we died of starvation, so I took it from my waistband and gave it to my aunt and uncle who traded some of it for Ramen Noodles. They used the small pot they brought, heated some water for the noodles, and gave it to the four of us children. While we scooped out noodles with our fingers and slurped up every drop of the tasty meal, the equally hungry adults sat and watched. They'd wait until another day to eat.

In the coming days, we discovered another boatload of refugees who arrived the day before we did. More and more people found their way to the island nearly every day.

A small stream offered the cleanest water we could find, so we used it to rinse the sand and sweat out of our clothes, then draped them over some bushes to dry. With only one change of clothing each, my sister and I made daily trips to the stream for laundry duty. We also found some buckets and used them to gather water for drinking and bathing. The few muddy steps from the bank of the stream down to the water proved a challenge, and we often slipped down. We had to stop and laugh at each other before we climbed down and refilled our buckets. Later, someone dug a well making our chore a little easier and less muddy.

We sweltered in the tropical heat of Vietnam, but now we roasted in the equatorial heat of Indonesia. Shelter became a high priority. Everyone pitched in to transform a long pole barn-type building into smaller cot-sized dwellings. My uncle gathered and wove together some banana leaves for a makeshift roof to cover our "room" the best we could. As more and more boatloads of refugees joined us, we hung pieces of clothing, plastic, and sheets, for walls between the family sections.

Relief agencies came to the island and set up an orderly census-type record of everyone who came to the island. They instructed us to report to them periodically and gave us some canned food determined by the number of people in the household.

We worked together with our fellow refugees and shared what we had. Someone must have had some type of knife, or perhaps they borrowed one from an Indonesian, because my uncle cut down some small trees. He built a pallet using short pieces for legs with longer strips across it, tied together with strong vines. That at least kept us off the dirt and mud when it rained.

~~~

I don't know what the flies ate before we refugees came to KuKu Island, but when we arrived, they found us quite tasty and multiplied into huge swarms. Because of their overpowering presence, they obviously ruled the island, so we renamed it, "Fly Island."

Certainly not to enhance their life cycle on purpose, but because we had no bathrooms, when we needed "to go," we found a place away from everyone and covered it up the best we could with some sand or leaves.

At least most people did.

Some didn't consider if their "going" location happened to be near another family's shelter, or whether they covered it well. When a morning quarrel erupted, we usually guessed the point of contention without asking.

Eventually, someone dug a hole for the purpose, but the flies didn't get the memo and continued to torture us. After we finished our laundry and water chores for the day, my sister and I tried to escape the flies with a run on the beach, a natural gathering place for children to play. We squealed and splashed in the water with the other displaced children. The flies had no trouble catching us, but at least we could dunk ourselves in the water and have a fighting chance.

We searched the island for anything edible and used our hands to catch fish, clams, and small rodents. With plenty of sticks and tree limbs, we kept a fire going to cook any small animal we caught, and to boil water from the stream. Every week or two, my uncle reported to the relief-agency census and returned with more canned foods such as sardines and Spam. While thankful for the food, we learned the Indonesians had a taste for Spam, so we saved ours to trade with them for some fresh fruits and vegetables.

Together, we refugees developed our own economy as we struggled to endure one more day. Each family used their dwindling resources for the best opportunity they could find. One family had baking experience and bought flour from the mainland vendors. The man built an outdoor oven with rocks and mud, and baked bread. Others traded for seeds, planted gardens and grew some food. Still others bought livestock.

We bartered and bought bread from the baker and meat from a butcher and made Vietnamese bologna *bánh mì* sandwiches to eat and to sell to the new arrivals. With no electricity for refrigeration, we kept our hands in a perpetual wave over the food to keep the flies away and prayed we could sell what we made each day.

With everyone in the same plight, most families tried to help each other when they could.

Most.

Not all.

One family began making sandwiches similar to ours and tried to convince people our sandwiches had fly maggots in them, hoping to steal some of our business.

We searched for ways to get food and earn a little money. My uncle found a net and a place to fish. He used every spare moment catching and selling shrimp. We survived and saved every bit of money possible so we'd be ready to leave when a chance presented itself.

Even with Red Cross, World Vision, and Care International all helping, they could only do so much with so few workers in comparison to the multitude of humanity in need. There would be no instant fix. They had to document, process, and find a place for thousands. We had to wait our turn behind those in line ahead of us to be relocated somewhere. Anywhere.

Over a short time, a quarter of a million refugees came to this one island. We waited eight months to send a letter to my parents so they could know we reached land—not Australia, but Indonesia.

~~~

With such a great number of people and flies in one small area, and no quality control over what we consumed, parasites, bacteria, malnutrition, and starvation slithered into our lives. Abdominal pain and diarrhea became universal among us. We brought no medication with us and found no means to disinfect or quell any contamination.

The beast of dysentery sprang up and took root. Graves multiplied on the island as the toxins around us waged war. The whole family next to us became ill. We heard the pitiful whimpers from the matriarch of the family as she fought the monster for days. One morning, the sounds of her family members weeping told us the enemy won that battle. The gravediggers prepared her final resting place, and family members scratched her name on a stone to mark the location.

Separated only by walls of fabric, we shared our neighbors' sadness and sickness. At first, the pain wouldn't allow me to carry the buckets of water or help wash clothes. Then it denied me any food I tried to keep in me. I gave in to the fact I had to lie down and hoped the illness would go away on its own. "The enforcer" could fight off any bully.

So I thought. In reality, my scrawny body had no reserves to fight off anything, much less the vicious monster of dysentery, and it attacked me without mercy.

I set my mind to think of standing, walking, eating, and getting better, so I could help the family. After a few days, I drifted into faraway dreams of home and our cool wooden floor. I longed for the wonderful food we shared, the smells of the market, my siblings, my grandparents, my parents. If only Mẹ were there with me, she would have made a special soup for me, hovered over me, and force-fed me if necessary.

My body and soul both ached with pain I never knew existed. I hugged my bony knees under my chin and tried to restrain the brutal monster inside that contorted my intestines into knots. Unable to take any nourishment, blood and fluid loss took its inevitable toll. My little body simply couldn't defeat such a powerful opponent, no matter how hard I tried.

After I used up every ounce of fight left inside me, I didn't have the strength to sit up and let someone spoon a few drops of water into my mouth. The gravediggers performed their solemn duty on my behalf. The monster claimed victory.

I wondered how long it would take for Ba and Mẹ to find out I died and light incense for me. I hoped they would know I fought with everything I had. The monster did not have an easy match with me.

I prayed none of my family would ever find out how I suffered. Surely my aunt and uncle would spare them that. Just tell them I drifted off to sleep.

My uncle gathered enough money to buy the medicine to cure my misery, lifted my limp body up off the pallet, and carried me to the doctor.

One shot.

One hundred US dollars gone.
One life spared.
One empty grave that day.
One hope still alive.
One more day.

Chapter 7

For months we continued our fight against disease and starvation to stay alive another day. The tiny bamboo and thatch "hospital" room a doctor set up, equipped with a bamboo table and an oil lantern that hung from the ceiling, stayed busy with those who tried to fight against disease. The severely sick or injured came to this room for help from a doctor assigned there by one of the international agencies. He had no equipment, few supplies, but gave what he could.

Some days added graves. Some days added life. Cô Mười gave birth in the little hospital room to a son, Buu, then promptly returned to us after the delivery. My other aunt, Cô Sáu, gave birth to a daughter, Hue, that same year. Little glimpses of hope were delivered to our family in the midst of a bleak situation. Loan and I took care of the babies while our aunts worked every day making bánh mì sandwiches to sell.

~~~

One day, when my uncle returned from a regular census

update visit, he brought us the ordinary canned goods and rice, but he delivered it with an unusual smile across his face. This time he brought back more than food, he brought good news—the news we waited so long to hear. After almost a year in the refugee camp, finally, our name came up on the list. A Catholic organization would help us begin the process to relocate, and we had a date to return to start the process. This news brought more life to our tired bodies than any Spam could ever deliver.

The agency would initiate the process, but before we could relocate, there had to be someone in that country to personally help us—a sponsor. Talk among our fellow refugees helped us learn some things would help or hinder our prospects. If we displayed evidence of any chronic disease, especially tuberculosis or asthma, that would delay our placement.

We also learned the younger our age, the better we looked to potential sponsors. So, we decided to add two years to our actual birth date, making us appear two years younger.

The relocation process continued ever so slowly. Our hope strengthened because the international community knew of our plight. But how much longer could we stay alive in these conditions?

My aunts and uncles talked about how much money we might need, how much we had saved, and how many more sandwiches we needed to sell. A fresh spirit of hope grew within us that our dreams could become reality. We did all we could to keep our frail bodies and hopes alive as the weeks and months crept along, day after hungry day.

On the day of our interview, we waited in a long

line and practiced our pretend birthdates. The agency representative reviewed our basic information and asked about our background. Because my uncle, Duồng Mười, served in the military and survived the re-education camp, he had priority to choose where he wanted to start his new life. His first choice, the USA. Most refugees wanted to relocate to the Land of Opportunity, which made the list extremely long, but with his priority status, we had reason to hope.

They asked, "Do you have any other relatives we could contact who might be willing to sponsor you?" Cô Sáu and Ông Bi, who previously lived in Saigon, had a nephew in Switzerland who might be willing.

The agency contacted the Swiss relative who happily agreed to sponsor them. With that offer available, they had to decide whether to leave while they had a chance or wait for an opportunity to open for America. After enduring so much and waiting so long, they decided to go to Switzerland. We could die waiting for the possibility of going to the USA. So, I hugged Cô Sáu, her husband, and infant daughter a final time before they left to relocate in Switzerland.

About a month later my uncle returned from a census check-in with food and the smile we saw once before. He brought good news again. They found a sponsor willing to take us in the United States. With a sponsor, the American Embassy could initiate the immigration paperwork to relocate us.

Once again, Loan and I rehearsed our pretend birthdates with each other and made sure we presented ourselves as healthy as possible for this all-important interview. I asked, "Do you think we might go to New York City? Maybe California?"

She added, "or Chicago, maybe? Do you think we will have rice and soy sauce there?"

"Of course. Everyone has that." I laughed. "What about the clothes? In Saigon we saw people wearing khakis and jeans. Do you think people in Chicago wear things like that instead of our type of clothes?"

"Well, it is cold there. They might wear coats and heavy clothes all the time in America."

I added, "I hope we don't freeze. What will school be like? Remember that man who lived near our school? The crazy man?"

Loan jumped in, "That man who shook all over and talked to himself? He scared us so bad."

"I know. Every time he came outside, we all screamed and ran into school. Someone told me that he shook like that because he worked at a slaughterhouse, and his tremors were his punishment for killing all those animals."

Loan's eyes narrowed. "I hope they don't have anybody like that there."

"He was probably harmless," I replied. I'm not sure I convinced either Loan or myself of that.

~~~

Galang

We packed up our belongings for a short boat trip to a different Indonesian island, Galang, the last stop before relocation. Our hearts swelled when we saw paved roads and shelters with real walls.

The Indonesian language is completely different from our own, but through motions and gestures the Indonesians showed us where we could stay and pointed to the one faucet available for clean water.

Good news—we had access to clean water instead of water from streams. Bad news—it would only be available from one faucet at certain times of the day.

Realizing the treasure of clean water, we fashioned a reservoir from some logs we laid in a circle and found a rubber mat to line it, making a little pool-type holding tank for any water we retrieved. At the "water times," my sister and I each carried pails in both hands to the water source. We waited in line, filled our pails, then took them back to our shelter and dumped it into the reservoir. Our feet trudged down the path back and forth, filling and refilling the pails as long as the water remained turned on every day.

In Galang, we not only had shelter and clean water, we also had access to medicine and food—real, uncontaminated food—along with access to representatives from many different countries who came to help this homeless mass of refugees.

Over the next few months, they assigned us each a number, took our pictures and lined us up for examination by doctors from Sea Sweep, a medical organization with World Vision. We declared our pretend birthdays with as much confidence as we could muster. They checked us again for parasites and contagious diseases, then immunized us against polio, measles, and tetanus. They also started us on treatment for tuberculosis, which continued even after we reached the United States.

After all the boxes on the official forms indicated we carried no communicable diseases, we boarded an airplane for the first time in our lives. An airplane with cold air blowing on the passengers. Who knew such a thing existed?

First stop—Singapore, where they quarantined us for a week inside a barbed-wire camp. Although it gave the impression of a prison, they treated us well. We ate a delicious meal of chicken cooked with lemongrass that reminded me of a dish my mother often prepared. Real food like this had become only a distant memory. We savored every morsel and the recollections the dish aroused. I wished Mẹ could see me, ready to start this journey. If only I could tell her we were safe and on our way. See her smile. See her wave to me.

Even after a good meal, long-term malnourishment took its toll. We laid our heads on the table to gather energy for our next interview or meeting, wanting to be ready for whatever hurdle they had for us.

~~~

Because we would need warm clothes to survive in the United States, some relief workers took my aunt and uncle into town by bus to buy some appropriate clothing to replace our lightweight Vietnamese clothes. With the money earned from selling bologna sandwiches and shrimp, Cô Mười and Dượng Mười bought us each some warm clothing to take to the cold country.

We proudly became owners of some heavy wool turtleneck sweaters while we waited for all the papers to be finalized. CARE International even provided us a sturdy white bag, emblazoned with their logo in bold blue print, for our precious new clothes, and threw in a few toiletries for our journey. Oh, how Ba and Mẹ would love to see me realizing their dream.

On the bus back to the camp, Cô Mười's bag couldn't be found. The bag held no importance itself, but it held the most valuable thing we had—the paperwork that documented our legal refugee/immigration status—the papers we'd waited for months and months in the refugee camp to attain. The papers that would allow us to start new lives in the United States. Without them, what would we do? Where could we go?

I couldn't even imagine. There is no word to describe the level of panic and hopelessness of that moment. They had to be found. How could we have come this far to have to start all over again? Would it even be possible to start the paperwork a second time? Why would someone take our things? Our hearts, so filled with hope, suddenly echoed with cries from hollow chambers of unbelief.

Strangers helped with the search. An angel in disguise checked inside a dumpster where the pickpocket had tossed our papers—trash to the thief, but priceless to us. This angel retrieved those treasured papers and returned them to us. Hope was a fragile thing, but it remained intact that day. At least they didn't get my sweater.

Reunited with the precious papers, we continued our journey. Our dreams might actually come to pass and we might live to see them.

When all the embassy officials from all the countries were satisfied with all the refugee/immigration paperwork, Loan, my aunts, uncles and cousins and I finally had permission to head to the United States of America.

Eight little Vietnamese refugees didn't have much except each other. But we had hopes and dreams. We had precious paperwork and heavy wool sweaters tucked in our brand new white and blue bags, packed and ready for new lives in the Land of Opportunity. The United States of America.

Chapter 8

July 1980

During the flight I tried to imagine what this new land might be like. Would there be a river anything like the Mekong? Would we be able to catch fish there? Would mangos and guavas grow in the neighborhood?

Would my new home have accordion doors and padlocks to keep out strangers? Would the windows have bars to keep out intruders and animals? Would we have to make or find a mosquito net to cover us at night?

Would it be as cold there as the inside of our freezer where we made ice? What would it be like to catch snowflakes as they fell? Would the snow have the same healing properties as the rain? Would it ever be warm enough that we could play in the rain?

What would their food be like? Would their rice be red or white? Would we even have access to food? Would there be a fresh market nearby? Would we have to walk a long way to get there?

Would I be disappointed and wish I were back home in Tân Châu?

Would my non-Vietnamese husband be there? How would I meet him? Would anyone there ever love me the way my parents did?

Our feet first touched American soil in the Seattle airport—the gateway to a new life. After the flight, we sat at a table to rest. While we waited, a lady with a basket over one arm walked over to our table. She smiled at me, then reached into her basket and picked out the most beautiful apple my eyes had ever beheld. With an outstretched hand, she raised her eyebrows to ask if I would accept the shiny red gift.

I opened both hands to accept it and gave her a broad smile in return. I absorbed every detail of it before taking a single bite. The smell, taste, and sheer weight of that enormous Red Delicious apple remains vivid in my memory. My "spoiled little rich girl" life in Vietnam included fruit. But, the small tasteless little gems back home paled in comparison to this perfect, juicy giant of an apple, bursting with flavor. If this apple represented my new American home, it must be even more rich and decadent than I imagined.

The length of the next leg of our flight required meals to be served. First item they brought us? Milk. We never drank milk. Too rich. We got the point across with the shake of our heads and the push of our palms against the little cartons. The stewardesses brought us some apple juice and orange juice instead. We drank the juice, but found it quite different than the fresh juice we had at home.

The flight attendants came back with our meal served on a plate, instead of a bowl. Loan and I poked around the odd food spread over these flat dishes but found no rice at all. No red rice. No white rice. No broken rice. Not a spoonful of it. Only something smothered with gravy–yuck. I looked at Loan and asked, "How are we going to learn to eat this American food?" Her face bore the same perplexed expression.

I remembered that as the elder sister and the more experienced of the two, I had great responsibility. So, I straightened my face to a smile. With confident nods, I encouraged us both with, "We are pretty resourceful. We will find us some rice and soy sauce somewhere. We will get some fish sauce, then we can survive. We can do this. We can do this."

She nodded and smiled in agreement. We speared some meat with our forks, held it up to our mouths, nodded at each other one more time. In unison we put the food from our forks into our mouths. Neither wanted to be the first to break our agreement, so with encouragement to and from each other, we chewed and swallowed this strange form of food. A few cringes. A few shudders. A few forced swallows, but we managed to eat it.

Loan and I talked about whether our new home might be a bustling metropolitan city like Saigon, or a small thatch-roofed community in the countryside like where our grandparents lived and made fish sauce. What kind of people would we meet—business people or farmers? What kind of life could be waiting for us? We would have to learn a new language, a new culture, and make new friends. Both my sister and I were eager to try our hardest—willing, eager, and filled with excitement of all the possibilities that awaited us at the end of this flight.

~~~

Alabama, USA

God already placed our plight on the hearts of a wonderful family in Alabama, the VanKirks. They and other families within their churches pooled their money, rented, and furnished an apartment for us.

The cross-country flight finally drew near to our destination and my fairy-tale dream of life in the United States began to play out. Our first glimpse of the land of our opportunity came as the plane lowered below the clouds to land at the Huntsville International Airport.

Because Vietnam brimmed with homes, buildings, and people, I expected to see the same here. Instead, from my window on the plane, I only saw neat rows of lush green plants on red dirt below me. These fields seemed to reach to every horizon, but they contained no houses, no businesses, no markets, no people, and no water buffalo. How odd to see so much open space and so few homes and faces. Were we going to land in the middle of nowhere?

~~~

"Grateful" does not adequately describe the Vietnamese family who landed in Alabama that day. We knew little about America, other than tall, blond, wealthy people lived there, and it would be cold—everyone knew that—but more importantly we knew somebody cared enough to welcome us to Alabama. Alabama, USA.

Inside the airport, I saw no other Asian faces outside our family, which made it easy for the VanKirks to find us. Instead of meeting tall, fair-skinned, blue-eyed sponsors, to my surprise, Mrs. VanKirk had the appearance of an Italian. We wouldn't be the only people with dark hair in America after all.

They spoke no Vietnamese and we spoke no English, but they came prepared with an interpreter, Ann, from a local Catholic church. With Ann's help, we used smiles and gestures to personalize our introductions and express our profound appreciation to our American sponsors.

We carried our blue and white CARE bags, packed with our few belongings and the papers we needed, and proudly wore our heavy wool turtleneck sweaters in the air-conditioned airplane and airport. We had no luggage to gather—or anything to go in one, for that matter.

Before we headed out of the airport, Mrs. VanKirk frowned at us, then motioned toward the bathroom where she made us take off our heavy wool turtleneck sweaters. We had traveled in an air-conditioned airplane to an air-conditioned airport, so we didn't understand her insistence, at least until the airport doors opened, and we stepped outside into a near triple-digit, mid-July, Alabama steam-bath.

We loaded up into their car for the ride to the apartment they prepared for us. Our open-air lives in the tropics rarely needed windows covered with glass. Their car included glass windows, completely closed. An air conditioner blew cool air onto us. What opulence.

The smoothly paved American roads allowed us to travel quickly past what we learned were fields of cotton, to the nearby town where we would make our new home. After over a year of waiting, and a couple of days traveling, it only took us a few minutes to glide over the level black road and arrive at the small town where an apartment waited for us.

The VanKirks—one attended a Presbyterian church, the other a Catholic church—and their church families completely furnished an apartment for the eight of us to live comfortably. "Completely furnished" in Vietnam carried an entirely different meaning from the "completely furnished" we found in the USA. Instead of a cool wooden floor for eating and sleeping, they had carpet-covered floors, couches, cushioned beds in separate rooms, tables, chairs, and pillows.

The expense of electricity in Tân Châu made it out of the question to waste it on anything other than lighting. We used a wood fire for cooking and open windows for cooling. Here, glass covered every window, overhead lights lit every room, and cool air came from vents throughout the apartment. We were overwhelmed to find an electric refrigerator, an electric stove, and separate machines for washing and drying clothes.

A shower in Vietnam involved a scoop or two of water we poured over our head after we lathered up with soap. Here, unlimited warm water flowed from overhead, and the VanKirks had laid out separate soaps for washing our hair, our face, our hands, our clothes, and dishes.

At home, open shelves displayed everything. Here, the storage shelves all sported doors on the front. With glass over every window, we couldn't hear the outside noise. We looked at each other, and for some reason whispered about the quietness within the room, hesitant to disturb it.

Instead of a hole in the bathroom floor and dipping water from a basin to both clean ourselves and flush the waste, we found an American chair-like toilet with paper for cleaning up, and water to flush it all with a simple push of a lever. Plus, in the bathroom we found another area completely separate from the toilet to shower in.

Whew.

We had a lot to learn.

They motioned us to a refrigerator, pulled open one door, and exposed shelves of perishable fruits and vegetables. The shelves on the freezer side were packed with beef, chicken, and vegetables. At home, we added chicken to our rice for an extra special treat. Here, we had a freezer filled with chicken available any time we wanted it. Did this mean they had no daily market available?

They opened door after door of the kitchen cabinets until they opened one that revealed bags of long grain rice.

Rice.

Loan and I grinned and raised our eyebrows at each other. We would survive. Not just survive, we would live in a place fit for a king. It must be practically like the White House.

Unlike most Americans, we weren't terribly picky about what we ate. My cuisine had included snakes, grilled mice, sautéed silkworms—the texture of soft-cooked egg—and even spiders, deep fried and crunchy, dipped in pepper sauce, so I rarely balked at trying something new, unless it was covered with gravy. When we spotted a brightly colored can of something we didn't recognize in the freezer, I didn't mind giving it a try.

We guessed it was some sort of beautiful ice cream or sorbet and enthusiastically found spoons, opened the container, and passed it around so we could all have a bite. One by one we tasted it with the expectation of something wonderful. Our smiles quickly contorted into grimaces, and we rushed to scrape it off our tongues. How could Americans eat such a thing? We found out later we spooned frozen orange juice concentrate onto our unsuspecting taste-buds.

We had a lot to learn.

The VanKirks recognized our overwhelmed faces and came to our rescue. They tutored us on how to cook on an electric stove. One of our first lessons—how to cook oatmeal on a stove with an on and off button instead of a fire underneath. Amazing.

Mrs. Vankirk added powdered milk to the oatmeal and told us it added nutrients the children needed to grow strong bones. For a whole year they came every day and taught us how to operate these fantastic appliances, and transported us to various doctors, the health department for shots, and even to the dentist. Each visit brought the reminder to use milk to help nourish our scrawny bodies.

They introduced us to the American version of a market in an enormous building completely covered and enclosed. When we neared the entrance, someone, somewhere, somehow slid the glass doors to the side for us to enter. Curious about their hiding place, my sister and I searched around the corner to try to find them inside, then went back out again to see if we missed them out there. After walking in and out several times with no person or door handle visible, we decided to solve this mystery later and caught up with the rest of the family.

Inside, the VanKirks had pulled out a giant metal

basket on wheels and pushed it along with us. With no local vendors calling out to us about the quality of their goods, we wandered wide-eyed through the quiet American grocery store in air-conditioned comfort, past stacks of meat from livestock already slaughtered, neatly packaged, and priced in electrically cooled bins.

Instead of carrying a basket over an arm, as we found things we needed, we let our metal basket on wheels carry them. Aisle after aisle of shelves stacked with practically every kind of food we could imagine waited for us to choose them. The fruits and vegetables weren't as exotic and fresh as we enjoyed in Vietnam, and we found no dried fish or fish sauce, but the variety and abundance overwhelmed us.

At home we used everything over and over. Here, the shelves and bins were filled with toss-away paper and plastic items. The extravagant Americans paid for things to throw away instead of washing and reusing something they already had. We shook our heads at the waste.

On every aisle we saw something wonderful, far beyond anything we imagined, including many things we had never seen before. How could I ever explain this to my family back home? I wrote to them about this land, so full of food, open space, opportunity, and paved roads. We had not yet found any fish sauce, but other than that, we had everything we needed. More than we needed.

Except our family. I thought of them every waking moment. I hoped Mẹ and Ba didn't worry about us and wrote letters reminding them that I prayed I'd see them again soon.

~~~

One of the first goals for the family: find a way to make a living. So, my uncle Dượng Muối applied to work at a nearby chicken-processing plant. My aunt Có Mười stayed home with Buu until he grew a little older.

My sister Loan and I, along with our cousins Hung and Minh, enrolled in school that fall. Not long ago, I had bravely welcomed the adventure of coming to this new land, but now as I prepared for my actual first day of school in a country where so many things were foreign, fear crept in. Would it be anything like my school in Tân Châu? Would I fit in? Would I be able to make friends? Would I be able to communicate?

Back home in Tân Châu, I used my morning walk to school to gather my breakfast. I first stopped at our family bakery and got a split baguette. Then I strolled to a deli and bought some meat to put between the two sides. I leisurely ate my sandwich while I finished the walk to school, speaking and waving to everyone I knew along the way. Here, I knew no one, no one knew me, and I had no idea what to expect.

Because of our desperation to find a sponsor quickly, or rather have a sponsor find us, my paperwork still listed me as two years younger than my actual age of thirteen. My malnourished little frame concealed my secret when I joined a third-grade class.

With my first glance of my new American school, I noticed there were no trenches. They must not have bombs nearby very often. The windows were closed. They must use their American electricity for heating and cooling even in the school buildings. I took a deep breath, put my fears behind me, forced my face to smile and entered this unknown place.

Inside the modern classroom, I quickly surveyed

and found no other Vietnamese face in the room. A variety of light and dark-skinned people sat staring at me.

I smiled.

They smiled back.

My teachers went out of their way to welcome me, and they made sure we all were accepted equally without prejudice.

Instead of long benches and tables we shared in my Tân Châu school, here each student had their own desk and chair. For the first time, instead of our custom-sewn thin pajama-like Vietnamese clothes, I wore sturdy, store-bought, modern American clothes supplied by our generous sponsors. They even had closed-toed shoes for us. I actually fit right in with the class, and they made me feel at home.

Instead of going home to eat at midday, American schools offered students lunches prepared in a kitchen there. They even had a lunchroom with tables where we could sit and eat. Someone told my aunt and uncle we qualified for a reduced-price lunch.

At first, we accepted the meals and ate there, but my sister and I talked about it at home. It embarrassed us to take food without paying, so we stopped eating lunch. We were grateful, but deeply ashamed. Our family did make use of food stamps and received blocks of cheese and other commodities for a short time, but only until my uncle made enough at the chicken plant for us to live on.

Having only been in the country a short while, I still knew no English, so, every day a teacher brought me to a speech-therapy class that helped me learn how to pronounce American words. The more I tried to learn, the more I began to enjoy school.

After school, Loan and I sat in our air-conditioned apartment on carpet-covered floors and discussed our family back in Vietnam. "What do you think they are doing right now?" she asked.

I answered, "Do you think they might be swimming in our favorite spot in the Mekong? It might be safe there now."

"No. Too dangerous," Loan replied from behind furrowed brows, then giggled. "Maybe they are putting barrettes in little brother's long curls like we did."

I joined in the laughter at the thought of his plight. Poor guy, surrounded by five sisters. Well, three now. "I wonder how tall he is now. I'm sure he has grown. What do you think they are having to eat tonight? Wouldn't you love to have some of our grandmother's red rice?" We both rolled our eyes in remembrance of her marvelous red rice.

"Can you imagine what Mẹ would think of the American market? Inside, with so much food already packaged."

"And she wouldn't have to wait for me to pluck chicken feathers." I laughed. "Wait until they get here and see women driving cars." We giggled at the thought of their faces if they saw such a thing.

"I hope they're not worried about us. It's already been so long since we saw them, and we probably won't get to see them anytime soon. Do you think they'll be all right there? Will they be able to survive? What if Dengue Fever breaks out again? They wouldn't have money to see the doctor. Why did the war have to come? Why did the new government have to take everything? Why do they have to stay on the other side of the world, instead of coming here with us?"

We couldn't comprehend how a government robbed so many of so much. Our selfless parents gave everything to provide us a chance. We were thankful for the safety of our new home, but still ached from the great emptiness in our lives where our family should be. We couldn't come home from school and tell them about our day. We couldn't hear their voices or share a meal with them. They were on the other side of the planet.

Two little girls so far away from home, and we couldn't be brave all the time, especially when cheated of our greatest treasure, our family. My sister and I tried not to cry. We'd already dealt with so much in our short lives as bravely as we could. But in the privacy of our room, when we could no longer hold in the deep grief for all we had to leave behind, we allowed ourselves to shed tears.

After a good cry, we renewed our determination to honor our parents' great sacrifice and make them proud. We came from a long line of strong and courageous people. Crying about it wouldn't make it happen. We dried our faces and encouraged each other to be strong, make good grades, get good jobs, so we could save money to bring our family here.

We would find a way.

We had to.

~~~

Our sponsors invited us to attend a Presbyterian church with them. We even cleaned the church for a little extra money, but we understood too little English at that time to comprehend what they believed. I never discovered who, but that first year, someone put our names on a

Salvation Army Angel Tree.

My classmates talked about Christmas, and we saw decorations around town, but in Vietnam, we knew nothing of the holiday. Our first Christmas morning in America, we woke to find a Christmas tree assembled and decorated in our living area. Around it lay mesh bags filled with candies and gifts. Mine included a Strawberry Shortcake doll. An enormous bag of perfect oranges made it even more delightful. It might not have been the fresh tropical fruit from our little market, guava from our neighbor, or fresh mangos from my grandfather's tree, but what an unexpected and welcome treat.

This tropical island girl, who had never lived in temperatures below sixty degrees, experienced her first taste of snow that year. White flakes floated in the sky and formed a fluffy blanket over the land. We children were excited to get out and explore this fairy tale of a scene, but my cautious uncle rushed home from his late shift at work to drive us to school so we wouldn't have to walk in it.

I couldn't reach out and pull my siblings to the window to watch the snowfall with me, or even pick up a phone and call my parents, so I tried to express my happiness to them within a letter. Without adequate words to describe the magical snowfall, I included a picture and tried to explain it the best I could.

The first part of my adventure leaving Vietnam failed to fulfill any part of my dream. But this part, my life in the United States, far exceeded any expectations I'd ever hoped for. I still had no real way to share the abundance and freedom of this place. I wished I could somehow open a window and let them see into my life here, but a letter had to do—for now.

~~~

With wonderfully compassionate and patient teachers, this new language began to make sense. Able to communicate with those around me other than family, for the first time I enjoyed school. With new passion, I tested out of fourth grade altogether, and they placed me in the fifth. This little immigrant girl skipped a grade her first year in a new country.

The more I comprehended the words on the pages, the more I picked up books for the sheer enjoyment of the stories inside. I read accounts of history, royal tales of princes and princesses, yarns of fiction and nonfiction—anything I could get my hands on. To motivate the class to read more books, our teacher used the Advanced Reader (AR) program and set up a contest. For each AR book we read, she added a section to our individual paper bookworms on the wall. Guess whose bookworm had the most segments? I won the AR award for reading more than anyone else in my class.

I wrote my parents to let them know their daughter, who would have failed school that last year if I hadn't left Vietnam, skipped a grade in the United States and won a reading award. I told them how well we were all doing, assured them they made a wise choice to send me here, and reminded them how much I appreciated their decision and sacrifice. We still faced difficulties, but I hoped they were proud of me and satisfied they made the right decision.

They carefully responded to my letters in generalities, knowing Communist officials read each letter that left the country. Sometimes Ba started the letter, and each sibling added a sentence or two about what they were doing. Other times one person wrote the whole letter. My sisters and brother always promised me they worked hard in school, reminded me they missed us, and hoped to see us again someday. Letters helped me not feel completely isolated from them. They also reminded me how much my eyes longed to see them again in person, and how my ears missed their voices chatting about their day-to-day activities.

~~~

My aunt and uncle took good care of us and believed in not merely surviving but working toward a better future. Both Có Mười and Duồng Muối worked hard and saved their money any way possible while still providing for us.

We shopped at thrift stores and learned to sew some of our clothing in order to live as frugally as we could. Slightly bruised vegetables and fruits were always available to avoid paying full price. Deli items reduced because they were one day past "best by" date made great meals. We purchased meat and bread items and promptly secured them in our "deep freezer" treasure chest. Since we were so malnourished, our sponsors encouraged us to add more milk to our diets, though it never set well on my stomach.

After a few years, my aunt and uncle enrolled in classes at a local community college and earned electrical-technician degrees. With that degree, they landed jobs at local industries and brought in a much better income, plus insurance coverage.

While they were at work, Loan and I took on the responsibility for preparing dinner and taking care of our cousins, Hung, Minh, and Buu. We decided the menu the night before, laid out some meat to thaw while we were at school, then cooked it when we returned home from school.

My uncle and aunt worked long hours and saved everything possible. Eventually, they saved enough to buy a Chinese restaurant in the neighboring metropolitan city of Huntsville. They began a family business in this Land of Opportunity and worked diligently to make it a success. Có Mười resigned her job and worked full-time at the restaurant. Dượng Mười kept his job at the industry to keep a steady income and valuable insurance.

We used our Vietnamese work ethic and business experience and worked seven days a week in the restaurant. My aunt and uncle even hired a seamstress in Atlanta to make us some traditional Vietnamese dresses to add an authentic atmosphere.

Loan stayed home and took care of the boys, and I waited tables, washed dishes, or whatever was needed as my contribution to the family income. They allowed me to keep part of my tips so I would have some spending money, but I didn't spend it. I saved it. I saved it all. I had to fund my college education, then get some kind of job in medicine or journalism to go back to Vietnam and see my parents and siblings. Big dreams required big money. In between waiting tables, I studied. I kept my books on a certain table at the restaurant so I could pick them up to study when I had no customers.

Through middle school and high school, my grades and confidence grew. Instead of not fitting in as I feared a few years before, I developed many friendships. In middle school, someone nominated me to participate in a beauty pageant, and the school voted me Miss Congeniality. I busied myself with my school and work and didn't write as much as I did when we first arrived.

~~~

August, 1987

A letter from Thu:

We are wondering how you are doing. I am in Saigon to see a doctor about some sinus trouble, so while I am here I am mailing this letter.

Did we tell you that Tham, Xinh, and Duyen all had Dengue Fever and Duyen had measles at the same time? It cost two ounces of gold for the IV and antibiotics and they were scarce because of the outbreak. Everybody is good now.

We miss you so much, because we haven't heard from you in a long time. We are still in school. I know you are busy, but please make time to write us so you don't forget Vietnamese. It will be good practice.

Remember to obey our aunt and uncle. Our parents owe them.

Dengue Fever? Thousands have died from that horrible disease, and I didn't even know they were sick. How did they manage to gather so much money? They still had to travel to Saigon to mail a letter, or at least have a better chance of it getting out of the country. The Communists must still filter through everything going in and out.

It hurt to hear they had been so sick, and to be reminded I had not written in a while.

A long while.

I didn't want them to worry about me, but it also hurt me to write about the wonderful things here, knowing how little they had there—especially when I had no way to bring them here. But I couldn't let myself focus on their situation. They were all well again. I had to concentrate on doing my best in school here, maybe even get a scholarship. The quicker I reached my goal, the quicker I could help them.

~~~

I allowed myself to entertain the dream of joining the band. My dream came true and I played the flute for a whole week with my high school band. But when we learned band required extra money—money we did not have—I pulled out. Extras would have to wait. After all, I had a goal to attain, so I returned my focus to my studies.

I would have given all I had to tell Ba and Mẹ face-to-face about my induction into the National Honor Society. The candlelight ceremony included a time to recognize both the achievements of the students and the support of their proud parents. I watched as student after student walked in the ceremony and their beaming parents stood tall and proud.

When they announced my name over the speaker, only awkward silence stood with me. That deafening silence echoed in the empty chambers of my heart. I stood alone and scanned the crowd—hoping against reason Ba and Mẹ were somehow there in the audience, somewhere in the shadows hearing and seeing this. If only they could have seen me in that moment, especially knowing how little effort I put into school before. If only the audience here could have seen their smiles and have known of the incredible sacrifice my parents made for me. I knew they would be proud. They were proud. They just weren't here to share my accomplishment.

I missed their voices, their smiles, their hugs. I missed being their "spoiled little rich girl." I didn't miss life in the new Vietnam. Life there would never be the same as before, and life here was so good. My next letter included some money, a little about the induction ceremony, and a firm renewal of my pledge to bring them here. I would find a way. I would see them again. I promised.

Only a year later, I asked a retired teacher—who had become a substitute grandmother to me—to stand in support of my sister at her induction into the same society. No need for her to be alone at such a moment of achievement.

In my senior year of high school, my former third grade and ESL teachers who knew my story and situation offered to take me on a shopping excursion. Someone nominated me to be in the homecoming court, and they said they were proud of me and wanted to do something special for me for this occasion. I came home with a dress, shoes, pantyhose, and the perfect necklace to finish it off.

I nicknamed the lovely black dress with a large white collar, my "Puritan dress." They even arranged a professional makeup application for me at Merle Norman. I rode in the parade and practiced my regal wave like the beautiful princesses I read about. My teachers told me again they were proud of me and all I had accomplished, and I believed them. It wasn't the same as having my mother, but their words and actions encouraged me more than they will ever know.

~~~

1989

Ba found a job working for a cousin at his import/export seafood business and wrote this letter:

I just received your gift of money and used it to buy gold. The business is okay, but we cannot deal in cash. We always hurry to change any currency to gold. Thank you.

We have learned that to sponsor some of us to come there, we have to give the government seven thousand US dollars per person. That is too much money for you. Think, if we had ten thousand dollars, we could open our own business and earn money for the whole family here. My cousin has connections in Hong Kong and Singapore to trade goods, so it could be a good business and income.

I had hepatitis for a while, but doing better now. How are you?

I replied:

I am working hard in school and will go to college soon, then get a good job so I can sponsor you. I might even become a doctor. I love you and I miss you. Tell all my sisters and brother I said to work hard in school. I will find a way to see you again. I promise I will.

1989

From Thu:

I just received your letter. I am so happy to receive it and hear you want to go to medical school. I know you want to sponsor us to come, but Ba said it costs a lot, so just sponsor Ba and Mẹ and the two youngest children. They are young and can adapt easier.

My parents hoped to get all the children to the United States but didn't want to burden us with the financial responsibility of sponsoring all of them. They reasoned the two older children could make a living in Vietnam until my parents could earn enough US dollars to sponsor them.

From Thu:
How are you? I didn't get into college, but I am taking English. I went to a private school. The teacher is from the US. His English is very good. Even the janitor there speaks English. The teacher asked us to listen to "Voice of America" every night before bed and come to school to discuss what we heard the next day.

Our sisters and brother are still in school. Tham is smart and gets all kinds of awards in school.

Vietnam is very open right now. If we have the money, we can go to another country to study, and they will allow it. I am learning English, so hopefully someday I can come to the US and study.

How is your school? When do you graduate? Is it racist in the US? How do people treat you in school?

To Thu:
Very good. You need to study English so you can communicate when you arrive. I will graduate high school soon, then on to college.

There is no discrimination here in my school. We have people of all colors, and the teachers and students treat us all the same. I have a lot of friends but miss all of you. Thank you for the letter. Keep encouraging our sisters and brother to study hard in school. I hope to see you again soon.

From a sibling:

I am in Saigon. Ba and Mẹ just came here and went to the beach. Now a lot of foreigners come to visit Vietnam as tourists. It is very open to visitors. If you have the money, come home and visit – just don't mention politics and you should be okay.

I hope you are okay. Stay in school, that's what our parents hope for.

Another letter:

Ba sent you a video and pictures. Have you received them? We haven't heard from you. We are doing good in school. Dad is partner with someone to sell general merchandise and goods, but it is not doing good.

I have started to learn how to embroider, but it costs a lot for thread. If you have some thread there, could you buy some for me? If it costs a lot, don't buy any.

The next time you write please send pictures of you. It has been so long we don't know how you look now. I guess you don't make a lot of money focusing on studying and finishing school.

To think a few years ago my family brought home a wheelbarrow full of money at the end of each day, now my sister can't afford thread.

Thread.

I had to get them to America. Too many years had passed without us seeing each other face-to-face. They didn't even know what I looked like anymore. I sent back pictures, thread, and a lot of love. They counted on me.

Chapter 9

My friend Adrian's father served in the military in Vietnam. When I met him, I made a point to tell him, "Thank you for helping me."

He responded with a puzzled look.

"You didn't know me then, but when you served in Vietnam, you were helping me and my family, so thank you."

His eyes welled up with appreciation and he nodded a "thank you."

For my senior prom, I again dressed up like a princess in a borrowed dress, this one green taffeta and strapless. While we were inside the school gymnasium, Adrian and her boyfriend left the dance. She knew the burden I felt of having my parents so far away, and my desire to see them and help them, and she felt a great desire to pray for me right then.

They left the carefree atmosphere of the prom and went outside to the park adjacent to the school. There they knelt on the wet grass in their prom clothes in the dark, and diligently prayed that God would lead me where I needed to be—college—and to what I needed to do. I don't know how long they prayed, but God heard and acted on those prayers. Actually, God had already been at work, and they got to be a part of His work that night.

The exact time they knelt before God, my future husband, John, whom I had not yet met, shopped at a local mall. While they prayed for God to direct me, John glanced down from an escalator, and his gaze landed on an Asian woman at the makeup counter. Seeing her sparked a memory in him from years before. While in Costa Rica, he spotted an Asian woman on a road in the distance and thought, "God, that's what I need." He finished his escalator ride, made his purchase, and though he didn't know it yet, he brought home a unique receipt, stamped with the time he recalled something planted in his heart years before.

Adrian knew nothing about John's Costa Rica vision, but thought we would like each other and wanted us to meet. Adrian and her friend attended a church event with John that Sunday, and she told John about me. When she told him that I would graduate from high school soon, John immediately waved his hands and stopped the conversation. He'd already graduated from college and worked as an engineer, so he shook his head and replied, "I don't want to meet a high school girl."

They quickly reassured him, "She's twenty-two."

John raised his eyebrows, shook his head with fervor, and firmly declined again with, "I sure don't want to meet a stupid high school girl."

They explained my journey as a refugee from

Vietnam, how I learned a new language and started over in elementary school, and he finally agreed to come to the high school awards ceremony in a few days and meet me.

That's all.

Just meet.

When my friends told me about John and that he planned to come for awards night, I didn't expect anything more than a casual friendship, and agreed to meet him. Still focused on my goal to get an education, find a job as a journalist, then return to see my family in Vietnam, I had little thoughts of dating.

At the awards night ceremony, I received a partial scholarship to the same local community college Cô Mười and Dượng Muối attended. I gratefully accepted this tangible reward for my years of hard work and focus. If only those who made fun of my leather satchel years ago could see me now.

One hurdle behind me, and college and job straight ahead, nothing could stop me now from realizing my dream and fulfilling my promise.

After the awards ceremony Adrian introduced me to John. The four of us drove to a nearby Shoney's, found a table and talked over dinner.

Talked and laughed.

A lot.

I never shied away from a dare, especially one to eat something. When they dared me to try the kale garnish from the salad bar, with no hesitation, I reached in, grabbed a piece, bit into the frilly green and pulled off a huge crunchy bite with my mouth. I returned the remaining part to its place, tucking the obviously missing section under a bowl. I chewed, swallowed, nodded, and pronounced "good" to their roaring laughter.

Struck by his kind eyes and his sense of humor, I talked to John for quite a while. He asked about my life, family, and experiences getting to America. He talked about his family, his work, and his recent mission trip to beautiful Costa Rica.

As strange as it may sound, after that one evening, John and I were no longer strangers, but so comfortable with each other he could have been part of my family. I believed he might be "the one." I think he realized it too, but neither of us spoke that thought out loud to the other on our first date. He gave me his phone number, and we said good-night. I left with a new direction in my heart.

Before cell phones were common, we made phone calls from homes or businesses. If the call to one area from another area occurred outside certain district lines, it incurred a long distance fee. His phone number and my phone number landed in that long-distance category, but he had a calling card we could use.

Vietnamese tradition requires the whole family approve of any suitor before a couple is allowed to enter a dating relationship. My aunt and uncle did not know John or of our meeting after the awards ceremony. As far as they were concerned, I had no boyfriend and would not be allowed to date anytime soon, especially not a non-Asian. Besides, they needed me at the restaurant every waking moment not dedicated to school.

I didn't mention my new-found friend to my aunt and uncle, nor did I mention the Senior Skip Day when I wouldn't have to attend school after lunch. Without their permission, I used the calling card to call John, told him about my half-day off, asked if he would like to meet me at the park for a few hours, and bring along the pictures from his Costa Rica trip. He liked my idea and showed up to meet me, even after the kale dare.

He showed me his mission trip pictures, then we compared our childhood memories. We both had loving families. He grew up playing ball; I grew up dodging bullets and bombs.

His father worked as a fireman, and his mother worked at a bank. My parents were wealthy businesspeople—at least before the war.

His family had cats who ate the field mice, and dogs for pets and hunting. We brushed mice away from us as we slept. The Communists ate my dog.

He grew up free to pursue whatever career he wanted as long as he was willing to work for it. In the Vietnam I left, work had nothing to do with our future. It was completely controlled by the government.

We found common ground in our love for family and the freedom and opportunities in this country. Laughter often punctuated this meeting as it did at our Shoney's dinner, and we decided to continue to develop the relationship. Without much free time, much less permission to visit in person, we wrote letters to each other. Real, old-fashioned, pen-and-paper letters. We got to know one another for the price of a stamp.

My aunt and uncle worked seven days a week at the restaurant, and so did I. When I finally told them about John, they said he would have to come to the restaurant if he wanted to see me, so he did. In all fairness, Có Mười and Duồng Muối were only being careful. They didn't know John or what kind of person he might be. He already had a big strike against him by being Caucasian. They couldn't let someone come along and do me harm, and they didn't want to lose a worker.

John recognized their reluctance toward him and tried to earn their respect. He wisely made a point to honor them by speaking to them before he talked to me, every time he visited the restaurant. But, they were not convinced we should see each other and discouraged our relationship. We discreetly exchanged letters at the restaurant. When John brought a letter for me, Loan covered my tables so I could go to the restroom long enough to read it.

So, while I waited tables, John ate Chinese food. He ate a lot of Chinese food in order to be available when I had a break between customers. Sometimes he brought his Bible to read while he waited and told me about what he read in the Word of God, but never pressured me to act on it. John even took off work as an engineer in the space industry to fill in when a dishwasher didn't show up for work at the restaurant—another element of his character, which spoke highly about him to me, but not enough to convince Cô Mười and Dượng Muối.

The more I learned about John, the more certain I became he and I would marry. In my perfectly good five-year plan, I graduated college, used that degree to take a job that would allow me to travel to Vietnam and see my parents. I simply added marriage to the timeline after I finished college.

John—ever the engineer—drew up a graph plotting out my five-year plan, alongside a one-year plan he had in mind. He compared the two plans on a timeline that

116

detailed how his income alone would be sufficient for us to save enough to sponsor my family, even without my income. Using his plan, I could go to school while we were married and we could still save toward the sponsorship. We could reach the goal either way, but we could have more time together as a couple if we married before I finished college.

He convinced me.

Now to persuade Cô Mười and Dường Mười.

About eight months after we met, John and I agreed he needed to formally ask my aunt and uncle for my hand in marriage. Because they spent their waking hours at the restaurant, it would have to take place there.

John waited until the restaurant had relatively few customers, took a deep breath to gather his thoughts and courage, promised to tell me about it later, then strode into the kitchen and found my uncle.

When he returned and we had a private moment, John told me about his meeting with Dường Mười. He greeted my uncle as usual and told him as sincerely as he could how much he loved me, that he wanted to marry me, and wanted his permission to proceed. My uncle listened and considered, then donned a serious fatherly face for "the talk."

Not the "No, you cannot marry her" talk.

The "birds and bees" talk.

I snickered, covered my open mouth with my hands, then held my breath to hear Dường Mười's response.

John continued with his imitation of Dường Mười's broken English, "You know when you get married, a man and a woman, they want to be together, and they want to have the sex."

John had to be respectful, so he did all he could to keep a straight face, while his soon-to-be Vietnamese uncle explained the facts of life to him.

Duồng Mười rambled about all the intimate marriage details he could think of that pertained to young married couples, and continued all the way through the challenges of middle-age, then older couples, while John tried to maintain a respectful face and eye contact. Satisfied he covered every detail of "the talk," he returned to the question at hand. Duồng Mười declared, "This decision too important for us to make. You have to get permission from her father. If they okay with it, we okay with it."

I removed my hand from my mouth and exhaled. One hurdle down.

~~~

We still only had communication with family in Vietnam by letter, so I now had to write the most important letter of my life. When I left Vietnam, I only had an elementary school education in Vietnamese vocabulary, and I spent the last decade trying to learn English. With such grown-up emotions to express in my native language, and my future resting in the proper wording of this letter, I asked the Vietnamese cook for help. He agreed to write something highly respectful, convey my love for this wonderful man, and include our request for their permission to marry.

Everyone needs a Vietnamese cook/poet for such times. We didn't have to wait long for him to pen a wonderful letter. He wrote a masterpiece, eloquently alluding to classical Vietnamese poetry of love, family, and marriage, showing my parents high honor and respect with our request. I rewrote it in my handwriting and sent it out by registered mail, and kept a copy in case it got lost.

Communist officials carefully scrutinized every piece of correspondence to and from Vietnam. This shuffle from one official to another caused the mail to be delayed by months, rather than the days we expected for postal delivery in the United States. My mind knew it would take a long time, but my heart couldn't resist sifting through the mail each day with the hope of a little blue envelope from Vietnam.

I tried to imagine where the letter might be. Perhaps it lay stuck under something neve to be found on a boat or plane. What if they never received it? What if an official tossed it aside? What if they didn't like the idea of me marrying a Caucasian American? Would they be mad? Would they be hurt?

Weeks, then months passed after my precious little letter left my hands. It made the nearly nine-thousand-mile trip to Vietnam, then passed through all the official hands and eyes. Then my parents' reply passed back through all the official hands and eyes before it returned to my side of the planet. Finally, a blue envelope arrived at my house.

I held the featherweight letter in my hand that contained the weightiest matter in my life and reminded myself how much Ba and Mẹ loved me. No matter their answer, they always had my best interest at heart. Their sacrifices proved that. I searched the outside for clues, sat in the nearest chair, and carefully unsealed the fragile blue envelope.

My practical and loving parents wrote of how they raised me to make good decisions. They neither knew

John, nor did they live in this society to know whether it would be right or wrong for us to marry. So, they relied on my judgment and trusted my decision in this matter.

I read the words again to make sure I understood correctly and sure enough—the wedding was on. Holding the letter in one hand, I grabbed the phone with the other and dialed John while never letting my eyes lose sight of the precious blue envelope.

When a click signaled me he picked up the phone, I interrupted his greeting. "I got the letter. They said they trust my judgment."

John took a few seconds to process my quick version of the letter. When he realized I meant the one from my parents, he replied, "I want to see it."

I laughed out loud and reminded him, "John, you can't read it."

"I still want to see it."

Bless his funny little heart. "Whatever floats your gravy."

Next, I showed it to my aunt and uncle who responded with little emotion. They weren't inclined to encourage my marriage to non-Asian John, nor were they thrilled to lose my help at the restaurant.

I moved on to another part of the kitchen and shared the good news with the cook who rejoiced with us and our love story.

~~~

April 1990

Letter from Thư:

I just received a letter from Loan. I was so happy I was shaking to open it. I waited so long to hear from

120

you. It had three dollars in the letter, but it seemed like it had already been opened—please don't send money this way—someone might take it. Thank you, thank you so much, but please don't send it this way. The rule is if you send money this way, someone has the right to take it.

I also got the picture of you, Thanh, and one of John.

I do worry about you. I was so young when you left that I didn't have a big sister to ask what to do—to do the right thing. I was just ten years old.

Ba and Mẹ are so busy. They try to make money to take care of family. I am the oldest here now and do everything I can to take care of everything for school by myself... and have the responsibility for our younger siblings. I have to be a good role model for them.

I couldn't even send a few dollars in the mail to them. Even though I longed to hear from them, it still broke my heart to read between the lines about their situation and be so far away. But now I had to focus on my wedding, then college, then how to get my family here—the sooner the better.

My aunt, not even vaguely convinced marrying an American would be the best for me or their restaurant, decided to make a quick trip to Vietnam. Cô Mười quizzed other Vietnamese in the area about traveling and she learned with the right "connections," the legal restriction to travel to Vietnam could be navigated. She contacted someone who specialized in such things and purchased a visa. With a friend in tow, she traveled to Vietnam to make a case for my lack of judgment and brought a letter back with her.

May 18, 1990

Dear sister,

Cô Mười will bring this letter with her when she returns to the USA, so I write this letter to send with her. I want you to know on the day we came to the airport to greet our aunt, we were so happy. When she came out from airport, I came to hug her and almost cried. She hugged us all and cried.

Her friend who came with her asked, "which one is Thanh and Loan's father?" We pointed to Ba. She came over to Ba and told him, "your daughters miss you so much." I couldn't hold back anymore and I cried. I told Mẹ what the lady said, then she cried.

The first few days Cô Mười couldn't sleep and we talked about life in the USA. She mentioned about sponsoring the whole family and starting the paperwork.

Do you really want us to come and stay with you? Ba said that the paperwork will take a while and it will not be easy.

She also brought money from you to Ba. We don't know what to say except to say thank you, John and Thanh. She also gave me money, and the money to give our brother and sisters.

She said you might come here, but that costs a lot of money. I think you should save your money for your wedding.

If paperwork to sponsor us doesn't go through, just save so that you have enough money to come visit.

The picture of the two of you is very beautiful. We love it.

We love the tee-shirts with our name on it. But we

are afraid to wear them because it shows our name, so we will keep them as a souvenir. We sent you a bracelet for your wedding. Cô Mười will bring it with her to you."

A few weeks later, this letter from Ba:

May 15, 1990

Your aunt arrived. Your uncles and cousins and I went to pick her up. Everyone was happy and cried because we have been apart for eleven years. We thought we might never see her again. Went to her husband's hometown and stayed two days, then we came back to Saigon.

Loan, after Thanh marries you should stay and live with your aunt and uncle, not with Thanh. Wait until we come over there. Focus on school first. Talk to Cô Mười and Duồng Mười about staying with them.

Thanh, we send wedding gifts to you. A necklace and bracelet from me and your mom and a plaque with the Dragon and Phoenix. Give my greeting to your sponsor. After talking to aunt, your mom decided to come to US. Send my love to John and his family.

The Dragon and Phoenix are the perfect couple in Feng Shui. The Dragon is *yang* while Phoenix is *yin*, and they complement each other in perfect balance. When he included this plaque—this symbol of a harmonious and happy marriage—he relayed his blessing for our marriage.

~~~

John attended a men's group at a Friday morning breakfast and prayer meeting. He asked for them to pray my aunt and uncle would give me a Sunday off work so I could attend church. He also asked they pray I would hear and respond to the gospel message.

Sunday off? Sounded impossible to me, wedding or not. They would never do that, especially while Loan took advantage of a scholarship and studied in a different town. They couldn't run the restaurant with both of us away.

Impossibilities didn't stop the men from his church. They prayed diligently and the whole church joined their prayer. When Loan surprised us and came home for the weekend, Có Mười and Duồng Muối agreed to give me a day off for planning our wedding.

My family didn't attend temple, but still embraced a Buddhist philosophy. We burned incense on an altar to Buddha in remembrance of the dead and kept a Buddha of protection at the entrance to our home. We had an understanding of a god out there somewhere and a life after this life. In order to live well and be treated well in the next life, we needed to live well and treat others well in this one.

However, the perception of being a good person and treating people well trumped actually being good. The perception allowed us to establish our own moral compass, so being good meant whatever we wanted it to mean. Much of the perception of good or bad behavior revolved around how we treated our family members, elders, and fellow human beings, with any accountability determined by our own conscience.

When a family member misbehaved, rather than call attention to the bad conduct and cause embarrassment or shame to the whole family, family members ignored the misbehavior. It never occurred to me they were, in effect, enabling the bad behavior rather than establishing a firm right and wrong. At the time it seemed a good way to grow up—be nice to people.

I had been inside a Christian church and even attended Christian services before John invited me to go to church with him. My aunt, uncle, cousins, sister, and I all worked together to clean the ornate Presbyterian church Mr. VanKirk attended and the even more elaborate Catholic church Mrs. VanKirk attended. The services were solemn and reserved ceremonies with the robed choirs, but the congregations were polite.

When John and I arrived at Austinville Church of God for the morning service, I wondered about the lack of ornate trappings like the other churches I attended. When we entered, I found the simple brick exterior cloaked an equally simple interior.

Instead of hushed tones and solemn stares, the members here engaged in lively conversations and welcomed me with hearty greetings. The congregation served as the only choir. They unashamedly prayed out loud, proclaimed "Amen" to emphasize their agreement with parts of the message, and clapped their hands during the service. I'd never seen anything like it.

After the service, the pastor and the congregation went out of their way to welcome me as if they already knew me. It was good to spend time with John in this happy place with such open and friendly people.

The congregation continued to pray.

John and I came back that Sunday night for the evening service. In the welcoming open atmosphere, God spoke to me. Neither the pastor nor John pressured me to do anything, but a voice within my soul did. For the first time I understood God determined right from wrong, not me. I suddenly recognized my accountability to Him, rather than my own conscience. God's Spirit spoke directly to my heart to let me know He loved me and wanted to be part of my life. I realized I could not save myself and I needed Him to be my Savior.

The pastor asked us to close our eyes and bow our heads while he prayed. Then he asked us to raise our hand if we wanted to make a decision. My hand popped up. I don't know how it got there, but it did, like the day I saw Ba coming down the road for me and I reached my hand up in the air so hc could find me.

Then the pastor asked if those who had the courage to raise their hands would also have the courage to come down front to share our decision. When the congregation started to sing a song of invitation, I tapped John, motioned for him to move over so I could get out. I side-stepped out of the pew all by myself, on a mission to get to the preacher at the end of the aisle. Without a doubt, I knew something in me needed to change. I needed Jesus in my life; I needed and wanted Him to be my Savior.

After I passed a couple of pews, I heard rustling behind me and turned to see what made the sound. Behind me, the entire congregation lined up and followed me down that aisle in jubilation.

I knelt at the altar and prayed to God, baring my heart to Him with my desire to change, to know Him, and have Him in my life. The congregation surrounded me. They prayed in earnest over me and my life decision. I'd come to church that night expecting to meet the friends of my husband-to-be and left a part of a new family.

John and I worshipped together in the following months and grew even closer to each other. I still had a lot to learn about him and even more to learn about God. The only gods I knew about before were cold statues that sat motionless for our rituals. I never believed they could take action or could know me personally. It didn't occur to me that I could know the God of the universe much less that He could know me.

But, as gently as Ông Nội corrected me when I tried to take what did not belong to me, God began to teach me to seek Him rather than to act on my own conscience. I learned to speak directly to Him as a friend and genuinely trust His will for me in my daily decisions.

As if blinders were removed from my eyes, I looked back at times God had been with me long before that night. John's early thoughts of marrying an Asian woman, the timing of Adrian's prayer and John's reminder of the dream in the mall, were all the hand of God working things together for my good before I knew Him. When I realized that He put the sense of adventure in me to leave my home country, placed me in a riverboat when there was no room, held me safe from pirates, drew us to land, pulled me from the death-grip of dysentery, and provided sponsors who brought us to this place, it became clear God had been with me all my life. If He watched over me through all that, then He surely would never leave me or forsake me.

The following year, I walked the same aisle again—this time dressed in white—to marry John. Once again, many people who loved us both surrounded us and supported our commitment to God and each other.

I could think of only one way to include my Vietnamese family in this happy day: wear a traditional Vietnamese wedding dress. So, while I wore the customary white American dress for the ceremony, I also wore a Vietnamese wedding dress for part of the day. Those pictures let my family know that although we were still far apart physically, my family was alive in my every heartbeat.

Loan shared our happiness, but because she and I now lived apart for the first time, she naturally missed our time together. She stayed busy at the restaurant and kept focused on her goal to earn an electrical engineering degree. With all the space and rocket industries in our area, jobs in that field were in demand. We encouraged each other in our mission to reunite the family. The whole family.

~~~

Before I could sponsor anyone, I had to be a United States citizen—so I applied for citizenship and studied the *Daughters of the American Revolution (DAR) Manual for Citizenship* for the test. History already ranked high on my favorite-subjects list, so I eagerly and diligently consumed the material.

I wanted to count myself as a citizen of the United States that had already given me so much hope, freedom, and opportunity.

More than me and my desire, so many people on the other side of the world depended on me to help them escape the place with no hope, freedom, or opportunity. They had already waited over a decade. I needed to do this sooner rather than later.

The four-hour drive to reach Atlanta for my 8:00

a.m. interview required that John and I leave home long before sunrise. We kept ourselves awake by reviewing the constitution, the balance of power, the names of presidents past and present, and all the civics lessons we could remember.

I started the day with full confidence I would pass. I knew the material, but fears slipped in. What if I couldn't understand the question, they couldn't understand me, or I fell asleep? That could not happen. Too much hung in the balance. If I didn't pass, I would have to reapply and wait for the test to be offered again, while my family on the other side of the world waited. Again.

No. I refused to panic.

I pushed those doubts aside and got back to reviewing the material to keep it fresh. When the interviewer called my name, I stood to greet him. He promptly asked if I spoke English.

"Yes, sir."

"Okay. We have a two-part test. The first part will be oral. After that, a written exam."

I sat across from the test-giver ready for the exam that would change the lives of my family near and far. My heart fluttered, but I willed it back into proper rhythm.

This was it.

The most important test of my life.

Back straight, I readied myself for historical facts I had worked so hard to memorize, and focused on the gentleman in front of me.

"Ready?"

I nodded and took one more deep breath to energize my brain cells and calm all the others.

"Question number one: Who is president of the United States?"

Oh, good. An easy one. I looked him straight in the eye, and through my clearest, best Alabama/Vietnamese accent replied, "George Herbert Walker Bush."

I sat tall, proud of my response and waited for a nod or smile of approval.

Instead, his brows furrowed and his eyes looked puzzled. He turned his head a little to the side. My heart raced. My chest tightened—allowing me only short, shallow breaths.

Did I miss something?

Did he misunderstand my words?

What could be wrong?

He took a few seconds to look down, then back up at me before he asked, "He has two middle names?" and laughed.

My lungs relaxed and let me exhale a sigh of relief. I joined his laughter and easily passed the exam.

~~~

Visits to Vietnam by Americans remained illegal, but I still held to the hope that a journalism degree might get me over there with a "news assignment." I completed two years at the community college, then transferred to a secondary college to finish my bachelor's degree.

My heart yearned to see my family, but the long-term goal remained the same: to sponsor them to immigrate to the United States. It would be a costly undertaking, but God blessed us with the financial ability to sponsor the whole family. We completed some preliminary paperwork for them to join us in the United States.

When I became pregnant with our first child, my

priority shifted from finishing my degree to being a parent to this precious baby. I missed my parents and siblings so deeply I resolved to be there for my children, so I put my education and career plans on hold to give my family here priority while the immigration and sponsorship papers processed.

John and I bought a tiny eight hundred square-foot home and readied it for our soon-to-be family of three. I imagined if Mẹ were with me, she would have advised me about what I would need for the room and how to set it up. She would have taken so much joy in pampering me and preparing for her first grandchild.

Even though over a decade passed since I saw her, I could hear Mẹ reminding me to stay away from shrimp and shellfish and be sure to get my rest. She would have planned to stay with me after the birth and helped us get our family routine established. Mẹ would have done anything and everything to make my life easier. She would, if she were in the same city, or the same county, or the same state, or even the same country. But from over nine thousand miles away in a Communist country on the other side of the world? Impossible.

If only she could be here with me. If only they all could.

~~~

A week before my due date, contractions doubled me over. *Tennis*, I thought. Playing a round or two of tennis might help the contractions come more quickly. Only a half-mile to a local court, I decided to walk there and play a round of tennis with John. When the contractions intensified, we drove our recently-purchased nice, safe, family car to the hospital.

Twenty hours later, an alarm shrieked furiously by my bed. A nurse rushed through the door in response to the alarm and found the imminent danger—a significant drop in our daughter's heartrate. The cord had wrapped around our little girl's neck, sending her into distress. The nurse expertly coached me to turn onto my side, allowing the cord to untangle. No more waiting. The doctors decided to immediately deliver our six-pound, ten-ounce little girl. A few minutes later, they placed a beautiful blessing in my arms.

As much as I loved my husband, I still longed to hold Mẹ's hand and have her hold mine. I physically ached to have her with me, to share the joy of the arrival of our beautiful Katherine and my life here. Mẹ must have experienced the same overwhelming joy when she held her firstborn for the first time. Both elation and grief dripped from my eyes at the same moment.

Somehow—don't ask me how—I heard my mother's wonderful, beautiful, contagious, unique laugh right there in the hospital, clear as it could be. I thought I prayed for the impossible, yet I received two perfect gifts from heaven in one day.

A few days later, we were amazed they let us take this precious bundle home with us. We strapped her in the car seat of our nice, safe family car and headed home filled with a lot of joy, and well, maybe a little fear.

Chapter 10

By the time our precious daughter turned four months old, I had already spent more time away from my family in Vietnam than I did with them. After almost fifteen years away from them, I couldn't bear any more time apart. I needed to go to Vietnam and see them, let them see me and introduce them to Katherine. However, a major barrier stood between us and any trip to Vietnam. Americans could still not travel to Vietnam, and the U.S. government would not issue visas for our trip.

Legally, that is.

I asked Cô Mười for the name of the contact she used to get her visa a couple of years before, and John and I made arrangements to meet him in a nearby state. We found the address and pulled into the parking lot behind the snaggle-toothed neon *Va_ancy* sign of the little hotel. Inside the office, the clerk behind the desk put aside his odd-smelling cigarette and pointed to the hourly rates posted behind him. We signed in, paid cash, then found the room that matched the number on our grimy key.

When we opened the door, a wave of stale smoke—and who knows what else—greeted us. The roaches scurried to their dark corners. We turned on the air-conditioner to bring in some fresh air, or at least move some around while we waited. No part of the room appeared to have been cleaned in the last few years, so we agreed standing was our best option while we waited for the bearer of our visas. We used one finger to pull aside the curtains. It didn't take long for us to see more than we wanted to see.

Soon, our visa bearer drove up, knocked on our door, and presented us with the papers. He puffed on his cigarette while we looked them over. They looked good to us, so with no questions asked, we paid him for three visas to go to Vietnam. We opened our luggage to make a bed for Katherine to sleep in, kept our clothes between us and the motel linens while we lay down, opened one eye each, both ears alert and passed the night until time for our flight to leave the next morning.

~~~

We asked our church family to pray for the connections and our safety on our trip. Traveling in a country with no established relationship with the USA and no embassy would be risky. If anything happened to us, the American government would not come to our rescue.

We would need plenty of money for traveling expenses, plenty extra for "official one-time taxes" to keep us safe, and even more for the unknowns that always arise when traveling that distance for an extended length of time, especially with an infant. We pulled out the money in our savings account, took out a title loan on our nice, safe car and bought our plane tickets for the thirty-six-hour trip.

Knowing we were coming, my aunt, Cô Sau, who'd relocated to Switzerland, scheduled a trip back to Vietnam for the same time we would be there. She arrived the day before and stationed herself at the airport to welcome us when our flight arrived.

While we waited in line to go through security check, our daughter became uncomfortable in the heat of the airport and cried inconsolably. Cô Sau heard her and spotted us. She made her way backward through the crowd of people to reach us, like a basketball player "boxing out" an opponent. We shared a quick embrace. The rest of our sweet reunion would have to wait until we passed through all the custom inspections. She took Katherine to a cooler area of the airport while John and I waited our turn.

John nudged me and whispered, "What if our visas are rejected and we are separated from Katherine? The nearest US embassy is in Thailand."

I raised one eyebrow, tilted my head and reminded him, "We've got American dollars. It's okay."

Because Americans were not expected to travel to Vietnam, none of the required official forms we needed to complete to enter the country were written in English. Only Vietnamese, French, and Chinese. Already bleary-eyed from the long trip, and a decade removed from practicing my written Vietnamese, my brain refused to tap into anything Vietnamese at that moment. I could only tune into the crying child waiting for me and family close enough to touch, but so far away I couldn't get to them.

I redirected John to focus on the paperwork. Thankfully, he had enough brain cells working to rescue us with his high school French, and completed the basic questions on the forms. At least we hoped he answered the questions correctly.

The security guards furrowed their brows to let us know they expected to find something sinister or valuable. They murmured under their breath, fingering through our things. We submitted to every possible search and question until they could find no reason to detain us. We declared two-thousand dollars of the American currency we packed and were promptly taxed five-hundred dollars for bringing it with us.

People could not legally exchange goods for American money, but American currency had great value. So under-the-table transactions over the course of a decade had those US bills worn threadbare. We packed plenty of fresh bills that were eagerly exchanged in private.

The guards shrugged their shoulders, unable to find any reason to hold us. They allowed us to proceed, but their piercing eyes told us they'd be watching.

Watching very closely.

Unable to find our undeclared money, yet sure it was there somewhere, they stuffed our things back in the bags and scowled at us. Their fault. They didn't search the bottom of the baby wipes containers and the inner soles of John's shoes. We entered the country, my home country, safe with all our belongings.

Finally, I found my mother's face in the crowd. Her tear-filled eyes met mine and we fell into a long-overdue embrace flooded with her beautiful laughter.

For the first time since I left her as a barely twelve-year old child years ago, I squeezed my arms around my mother again.

I whispered to her through happy sobs, "I am so thankful to have you two as my parents. I am so thankful for your sacrifice, your amazing sacrifice. Now I have a daughter, and I understand a little better about how the love for your child gives you strength to act in their best interest, even when it comes at a high cost for yourself. I always loved you, Mẹ, but now I love you even more for the wonderful unselfish decision you made for me."

When we paused our hug, she held me by both shoulders at arm's length and looked me over head to toe. The twelve-year-old daughter she last saw walking out of her home, now stood before her all grown-up, and back home with her own husband and daughter. She shook her head, hardly believing her eyes. My heart barely contained the emotion when I saw Mẹ beaming at us with such joy. I tugged John's elbow, pulled him into our reunion, and proudly introduced my family to my husband. They offered their most polite handshakes and formal bows. John responded with American hugs.

My father still listened to the BBC broadcasts and shared the news he heard that day—Alabama had received a foot of snow. We laughed it off because when we left we had no snow, much less a foot of it. We found out when we returned to Alabama, the BBC still delivered accurate news. He knew before we did about the blizzard that came to Alabama that spring.

The whole family loaded into a van and drove to a Saigon hotel where we could talk privately. We booked the cheapest hotel with air-conditioning available, and found it located in Cho Lon—the Chinese district of Saigon/Ho Chi Minh City. Even the street signs were written in Chinese. The streets were littered with trash and screamed of poverty and mayhem.

John watched amazed as a little girl stopped in the middle of the sidewalk, lifted her dress, and urinated on the concrete. Someone in the group she walked with turned back, saw what she was doing, and stopped to wait until she finished. When she did, she skipped to catch up to them and no one seemed to give it a second thought.

"Well, that's different," he noted.

When we arrived at our hotel, the people in front of us stepped over a street urchin lying in the doorway to the hotel, lifting their bags high enough to avoid bumping him awake from his sleep. We followed their lead and didn't disturb him.

After we checked in and surrendered our passports to the hotel clerk for registration with the local police, we headed to our room. The stubby-legged tables and chairs in the sparsely furnished room prompted John to ask if this furniture was made for children.

I smiled and told him, "No, this is normal for adults here." We tossed our things to the side and looked for the air-conditioner control.

The electrical wiring that was stapled to the walls instead of threading through the interior of the walls concerned John. We turned on the air-conditioner despite his questions and shook our heads. "Don't worry. Normal."

While we waited for the cool air to flow, Mẹ did what she always did for us when we overheated, she took her granddaughter aside to bathe her tenderly in some cool water. It might not have been a champagne bath, but a treasured moment nonetheless with her first grandchild.

We juggled five simultaneous conversations, answered questions and asked our own. After we distributed the Alabama 1993 Football Championship tee-shirts we brought for everyone, they gave us a runway-style fashion show. They considered anything from the USA to be a grand prize, so they wore them proudly, even though they didn't know what an "Alabama" might be, but they were pretty sure I lived in one.

Everyone wanted to hold Katherine and have their picture taken with her. They passed her around from lap to lap, and took turns drawing a smile from her. The sweet chaos of our family chatter swallowed me up into a perfect dream-come-true. If only a dream, I never wanted to wake up.

Two of my sisters worked in Saigon and met us there, along with my paternal grandmother, cousins, and other family members. While we squealed, chatted, and hugged each other, my American husband nodded, smiled, and bowed. A lot.

The challenge of short furniture didn't compare to the one my tall husband met in the bathroom. Vietnamese bathrooms incorporate only one drain for both the shower and the toilet. Americans who are spoiled by having a toilet chair-type seat have a rude awakening when they realize there is no chair or seat— only a drain hole in the floor. He came out and looked at me as if he didn't know how or what to ask.

I knew the question and gave him the answer.

"Stand for shower, squat for the toilet."

My six-foot tall husband nodded and turned back around to challenge his knees to a new adventure. He returned with another concern—exposed wires in the shower area of the bathroom. "Wiring and water in the same spot?" he started his engineering quiz with raised eyebrows.

Everyone tossed up their hands, shook their head dismissing any concern, and assured him, "Normal. Is okay."

Normal for them, maybe.

My brave John hopped on a motorcycle with Ba to explore Saigon. He hugged a duffel-style bag across his lap that held our camera and cash, while still holding to Ba's middle. As many as ten motorcycles squeezed together side by side in what Americans consider a four-lane road. No one wasted anything there—money for helmets or space for impatient drivers. To make it even more interesting, several passengers held five-foot tall packages—anything from pigs to potted plants and everything in between could be balanced on one motorcycle.

At a traffic circle, John had a strange rush of impending danger. While they waited for their turn to move forward, he tightened his elbows near his side and patted the ends of the bag to make himself and the bag as narrow as he could. He took his left hand from Ba's middle and anchored himself to the motorcycle seat.

When their turn came to move forward, the school-age girl on her bicycle in front of them swerved to avoid hitting someone in front of her. Her handlebar grabbed the strap of John's bag and pulled against John and Ba. Because John firmly gripped the motorcycle, they remained upright, but she fell to the street. If he hadn't changed his grip, if he'd only held onto Ba, the two men and their motorcycle would have landed on top of the girl.

They stayed in place while hurried cars, bikes, and motorcycles swirled around them, focused only on their own destinations. Then, after the traffic cleared, the young girl stood to show them only minor injuries—a skinned knee, torn dress, bent handlebars, but no serious damage. They took her to a nearby walk-in clinic where someone cleaned her wounds, then they left her with some cash for expenses, and made a quick exit. We didn't need any negative police reports about our visit.

~~~

We retrieved our passports from the hotel clerk who took detailed notes of our travel plans. Required to provide full reports of all the comings and goings of visitors to the government, he filled out the forms and reminded us to stop and register at every province we passed through whether we planned to stay or not. A recent coup attempt heightened government efforts to keep track of all outsiders.

With our passports in hand, we left Saigon to travel to my hometown of Tân Châu. The police stopped us often for questioning when they spotted John's non-Asian face in the crowd. Everywhere we went, they immediately blew their whistle and pointed at him, demanding he come with his papers for an interrogation.

Although only about a hundred miles away, the trip to my hometown took several hours. Roads and bridges merited little attention from the current government that promoted their own pockets, rather than the general welfare of the people. So, instead of bridges, travelers relied on ferries to cross the Mekong. Because of the twists and turns of the river, and the lack of infrastructure, we ferried across at least three sections of the river as we made our way north, stopping in every province to register our presence.

The ferry, worn out like everything else in this country, packed as many as possible aboard. If they could have afforded to buy a roll—they could have wrapped some duct tape around the boat and improved the level of safety tremendously. John's concern prompted him to get out of the van and hold our daughter. If the ferry went down, he could swim with Katherine to shore.

While he stood on the deck beside the van holding Katherine, he noticed a beggar with a little bowl that cradled a few pieces of currency people donated for his food money for the day. Anyone physically capable of working, no matter how menial the job, considered it their honor and responsibility to earn a living. Those who had little abilities because of physical deformities or severe illness such as leprosy considered begging a last resort. This man whose foot twisted up behind his shoulder, let his appearance and the bowl beside him convict any tender heart. When the water lapped up and over the ferry to steal some of his money, John quickly trapped it underfoot before it slid overboard. The grateful beggar wove his way between John's legs to his errant earnings and glanced up to give John a Vietnamese thank you, "*cảm ơn.*"

~~~

When we arrived in my hometown and my childhood

home, the corrugated metal doors opened wide—just as I remembered—to embrace me and my family with a warm welcome. I walked through those doors and memories sprang back to life.

I stepped back into a world that required so much effort to earn so little, especially compared to the abundance we enjoyed in the USA. They survived on a government allotment the equivalent of a couple hundred US dollars a year—a reminder this government was neither of the people, by the people, nor for the people. In comparison, we lived like royalty.

The Vietnamese air that had filled my heart with such joy years ago now weighed heavily within my chest. In a few weeks I would leave this oppression and poverty and return to freedom and abundance in America, with no way to take my loved ones with me.

At least not yet.

The walls were clean, of course, but had not been painted in so long the concrete faded from one shade of gray to another. Living in America already spoiled me to the luxury of affording simple things like paint, while here my family worked for day-to-day survival. I brought hairspray, magazines, and shampoo to leave with my sisters who could not possibly afford such indulgence.

Finally, I gave John a glimpse of my upbringing in Vietnam. We climbed the ladder-type steps to the second-floor area and set our things in the room behind my childhood one. Unlike my former room, where my siblings still slept on the floor, this one had a bed. John spoke of the beauty of the uneven but smooth, wide mahogany boards. We always removed our shoes to come inside, so between the natural oils of our feet and the drips from years of eating our meals there, the floors were beautifully polished.

Before we collapsed for the evening, we spread out the mosquito netting over the bed and settled in for the night. The evening breeze came by to give us a proper Vietnamese good-night kiss. We thought our fatigue would allow us to sleep easily through the night, but John woke startled by the splattering and gurgling of the water faucet in the next room.

I told him, "It's okay. Just our water delivery for the day."

"Won't it overflow?" John questioned.

"Nope. Never does."

He settled back into his pillow only to wake to clicking sounds, like tiny tap shoes across the floor. He lifted his head to find the noise.

I patted his arm and whispered, "Don't worry. Just roaches."

"Roaches?"

"Shh. It's okay. Go back to sleep."

He trusted my assessment enough to lie back down but stayed close to the edge of the bed to keep an eye on them. Poor guy. I should have warned him.

In the morning light, he realized why these roaches made so much noise. They were four-inch long soldier roaches, clicking their heels on the wooden floor around us. He also gained personal experience in the magnitude of "residue" a giant soldier creates when squished. Because of the massive clean-up required, he decided the noise reduction from removing a single soldier from a whole squadron's nightly drill-team practice not worth the effort.

A six o'clock wake-up call blared out a "Yankee

Doodle"-type reveille, blasting in concert all around us from neighbors who defied the law and tuned into the Voice of America. They had their AM radio volume so high the whole neighborhood could hear the deep American male voice declare, "Good Morning. This is Voice of America reporting from Washington D.C.," and the news that followed.

For the first time in years, I woke up in the same house with my parents and siblings. I recognized the familiar sounds of rolling carts, clanging pans, squealing animals, and all the aromas that I experienced as a child. Due to erosion along the banks of the Mekong that swallowed several blocks of the city, including Ông Nôi's backyard, the market shifted inland. Now situated just outside my parents' home, the chợ trời would immerse John into life in Vietnam. I hoped his farm upbringing prepared him for it.

Once we were up for the day, John noticed red itchy welts on one hand—the hand that rested against the mosquito netting while he kept watch for the roach invaders. The mosquitoes took advantage of the diversion, reached their little needles through the netting, and drew out fresh American blood. I should have warned John to stay a mosquito-mouth length away from the netting as he slept. Too bad for his hand. Those Vietnamese bloodsuckers went home with full bellies that night.

~~~

Our presence called for a celebration. Celebrations called for feasts, and in our home, feasts took place on the floor. A long blue and white vinyl cloth stretched from one end of the room to the other to accommodate a couple of dozen guests coming to welcome us. My family had also laid out a celebratory feast here the day we married, while we partied on the other side of the world.

This time, we joined in the feast with men gathered on one end of the room and women on the other while we sat cross-legged to share our meal. Together, finally.

I don't remember everything on the menu that day, but I remember one thing: Mẹ's egg rolls. My taste buds had traveled near and far and never found egg rolls anywhere that compared with my mother's. I don't know how many I ate, not that it mattered. I had to make up for years without them.

John endeared himself to my father right away by presenting him with a tennis racket. Ba took him to the local tennis court—the one beside the pig pen, cesspool, and public execution area.

Above the cesspool, a rickety bamboo walkway led to a small half-wall box. From time to time people walked to it, disappeared below the half-wall and stayed for a minute or so, then left. John saw a man go toward the box, so he watched to see if he could figure out why people were interested in it. The man's head went down, and soon John heard a plop.

John understood.

How awkward that he stared at this poor man. "Sorry, mister," John apologized.

A pleasant surprise for John—in the middle of a country with dirt roads, someone at some point splurged to buy concrete for this tennis court. They even had ball boys who, after they took off their shoes, would retrieve any stray balls from either the pig pen or cesspool, wipe them clean, and return them good-as-new to the players.

Sort of.

A Communist official roamed around in the fanciest motorcycle in town. With full authority to do as he pleased, most people kept their distance and held their comments until the official moved out of hearing range.

Because John's appearance screamed "Non-Vietnamese" and his height and fair skin suggested the possibility of Russian heritage, people often whispered to one another when they saw him. They pointed and scowled a bit but retained a little curiosity because he didn't wear a military uniform. Their cold treatment ended when I stepped in and reassured them he was neither Russian nor Communist. Once they learned his American status, they immediately transformed into long-lost friends.

A bar near my parents' house hosted karaoke for two cents per song, twenty-four hours a day.

Twenty-four.

It didn't take long for John to consider buying a whole day's worth of karaoke to give us one day of quiet. Instead, we explored the city when we needed a break.

Not built for American-height, the awnings that covered storefronts often rudely greeted John's forehead. At night the awnings were even harder to see before making contact. To defend his head from awning attacks, he learned to keep one hand in an almost salute position to protect his head while we walked around town. He became acquainted with snake wine—bottled with a real cobra poised to strike—Buddhist temples, thatch roofs, and open-air everything.

One day as we toured the city, we came upon a

home that had recently burned to the ground. The family who lived there, friends of my family, lost everything. It stunned them when we gave them a few hundred dollars. A small gift for us, but an annual salary to them.

We took about thirty friends and family members to the fanciest restaurant around and ordered the best meals money could buy. The equivalent of seventy-five US dollars we paid to feed those thirty people posed no hardship on us whatsoever, but far exceeded their budgets. Their currency so inflated, (about 12,000 dong to one US dollar) it took us twenty minutes to count out the currency to pay the bill. The restaurant staff counted and recounted the money on a separate table, then carried it away in paper shopping bags.

I tried to imagine their lives before we arrived and after we'd leave. Ba and Mẹ remembered the days of earning a living, buying and selling freely, but the generation after me had never experienced that kind of freedom or the prosperity that went with it.

~~~

Before we left America, we bought a month's supply of everything we could think of for our infant daughter on this trip. Mẹ didn't grasp the concept of disposable diapers, and tried her best to convince us to reuse the diapers until I demonstrated they were paper.

My family also gathered around to inspect the extravagant food we brought for Katherine—small jars of baby food just for her. American babies—treated like princes and princesses.

Even though we tried to keep as much of her diet and routine as consistent as we could, Katherine developed diarrhea. After a few episodes, it became apparent she might be sick with more than a one-time or even one-day problem. John and I became concerned we would need to return home to her doctor in the United States if she didn't improve.

We told my parents about the situation and tried to prepare them that we might have to cut our trip short because of it. We called a local doctor to come, and while we waited for him, we prayed God would heal her and help us know what to do.

The second nicest motorcycle in town showed up at the front door, and the doctor who rode it came in and assessed Katherine's situation. He dug into his bag and retrieved something wrapped in crisp paper. He rustled the paper away from a few discs of activated charcoal and presented them to us as the remedy. We crushed them and fed the charcoal to her with some applesauce and waited.

The next day I told my family, "Katherine is so much better. We can stay."

~~~

Because of the continuing Russian influence, all students were required to take classes to learn some of the Russian language. Most wanted to learn English, but the Communist-operated schools had little interest in offering a course in anything American. Instead, they had to rely on private instructors for any English-language classes.

My brother Tham took private English classes in the home of a man who served as interpreter when American dignitaries came, before the fall of Saigon. Tham introduced John to the English teacher, who extended John an invitation to come visit the English class, so his students could hear his "good" accent. John gladly spoke for the class and received applause for his outstanding English pronunciation.

The English teacher proudly told John the names of famous Americans he met through the years and about his imprisonment after Saigon fell. Because of his fluency in English, Communist officials believed he posed a threat to the regime. He also openly professed to be a Protestant Christian. Those two strikes against him sentenced him to ten years or more in prison, six to eight of those years in solitary confinement under horrendous conditions.

He tried to reason with the guards about the absurdity of keeping him, an innocent man, in prison. But the Communist officials were so brainwashed they didn't know how to reply except with threats. After several years, a couple of the guards became a little more sympathetic to his plight, but told him to be thankful. He could have been treated like the American in the next cell, an American who had fought for their freedom, but was held and tortured in prison because he had tried to help the Vietnamese gain the ability to pursue life, liberty, and happiness. If only the guards could have seen how different their lives would have been with freedom.

While he served time in prison, the English teacher's wife had to find some way to make a living. When any family or business tried to help her, the government punished them and her. She contracted cancer and died. He eventually helped his children escape to the United States. John and I grieved for him, but also expressed our admiration for his amazing courage in the face of such great opposition.

~~~

We traveled to many parts of the country to visit relatives and show John the countryside. He kept his camera nearby to take pictures of interesting buildings, faces, bomb craters, and scenery.

The trip to the city where my maternal grandparents lived required a boat. No roads or bridges existed. Because of their seclusion, the people there had never seen a white face until John came to their town.

They flocked to see this oddity—a tall, fair-skinned American. He entertained the children gathered around him by picking up a pineapple and clearly enunciating *pine-ap-ple* for them to repeat after him. They practiced repeating the English word, then pronounced the Vietnamese word for it. He tried to mimic each syllable after them, but they found it hilarious that this man couldn't correctly pronounce such an easy word. They tried the same game with "banana" with the same result—howling laughter.

John photographed the neat thatch-roofed homes and the throngs of people who were intrigued with his presence in their little community. His high-tech camera allowed a view of the picture either in color or in negative form. He drew laughter at every gathering when he showed people their color photograph, then transposed it to a negative picture that revealed their black-toothed smile.

All this fun traveling and picture-taking drew scrutiny from those who were charged with keeping up with strangers. Certain government officials came to believe he might be in the country to provoke an uprising against the government by photographing government facilities for sinister reasons. After some time traveling the country and taking plenty of snapshots of all of it, the secret police came to visit us at my parents' home with the intent of arresting John before he could accomplish his criminal mission.

Ba quietly calmed them by telling them our story and assured them our pictures were merely those of interested tourists who visited the lovely countryside. After a heated discussion, they agreed we might not be spies. They pointed fingers and spoke to Ba in gruff tones of the danger of John taking pictures, especially of government buildings.

Ba understood and asked, "What could he photograph then?"

They shook their heads, raised their shoulders and finally decided, "Just don't take pictures of anything with a government flag on it, okay?"

Ba nodded, "Okay. No pictures of government buildings or bridges, no government anything. Okay."

They continued their warnings to Ba, "Remember, this man has to develop everything, every single picture."

Ba nodded in agreement with their every command.

"They will not be allowed to leave the country with any unexposed film. All pictures and movies must be viewed and receive a certificate before they leave. It is also not good for John or for the English teacher to be seen together. Not good for any of you. Tell him he'd better stay away from him."

"Okay. They will," Ba promised.

The secret police left, not completely convinced of our innocence, but at least they did not take us into custody. They probably thought the truth would come to light when we had our pictures developed, or they could catch us outright participating in an anti-government activity. Clearly, they would be watching.

We got word to the English teacher why John wouldn't be returning for a visit, and carefully considered everything in the camera frame before we snapped any more pictures. With each city documenting our location and so many suspicions about us—eyes watching with their expectations of wrong-doing at every turn—we tasted a bit of the oppressive conditions my family endured every day. We obviously left our "blessings of liberty" on the other side of the world. No US embassy existed here to call for help, should the Vietnamese government conclude we were guilty of criminal activity or even intent.

We thought back to every interesting bridge and building we photographed and realized they all had government flags on them. The pictures could be interpreted in nefarious ways by the guards. We worried a little about having to report to the agency that inspected our film, but Ba had lived under this regime long enough to have a plan ready.

As required, we reported to the government agency for our video film review and certification. The shelves behind the counter were lined with stacks of VHS tapes. Our camera had no such tape, but did have the capability to replay the recorded video and watch the replay on a small viewfinder screen on the camera. We handed over the camera to the official who propped it on the counter between us and peered closely at the tiny screen while the video played.

After a few minutes, Ba pulled out a cigarette and slid it over to the official's side of the countertop. Without so much as glancing toward it, the official reached up, placed his hand over it, slid it below the counter, and simultaneously pushed the movie into fast-forward mode.

A couple of minutes later, Ba placed another on the counter. It too disappeared and the video hummed in high speed. A few cigarettes later, we held our certificate of inspection for the video. We followed the letter of the law and had our still-picture film developed and acquired the proper certificate of approval from that agency.

~~~

John made many friends during the month we were in Vietnam and even learned a little of the language. He greeted people with "Hello, how are you?" in pretty good Vietnamese. He understood my mother when she asked, "Are you hungry? You want to eat some grilled pork chops with pickled vegetables over broken rice with fish sauce drizzled over the top?"

His response always the same, "Yes!" He still orders that dish from any Vietnamese menu when he finds it.

My family considered him an honored guest and tried to take care of him. They graciously saved and presented to him the most tender portions of the meals—the fish heads and eyes. With the most genuine plea he could muster, he tried to convince them they didn't have to do that for him.

Before we left, we were treated to a party where someone offered John some *chuột* to eat. He was willing to try it, but before he tasted it, he asked "What is it?"

The host tried out his English and confidently answered, "Moose."

John didn't grow up in Vietnam, but knew no moose lived there. He squinted his eyes, leaned in and tilted his head to hear the answer again and questioned him, "Moose?"

"Oh, yes. Moose." He happily nodded. "You know—like Mickey Moose."

"Ahh." The light came over John's head.

So, for the first time John ate mouse, butterflied, grilled, and served over rice, of course. He concluded it tasted like squirrel.

~~~

Xinh told me that after Loan and I had been gone several weeks, she and Thư came back home. Something was wrong because the front door that should have been open was closed. Inside, a woman she didn't recognize sat in the hammock, crying. Mẹ had hardly eaten or slept, and had lost so much weight after we left, she was unrecognizable to her own daughter.

Mẹ couldn't bring herself to leave our house for at least a month. It should only have taken the boat a few days to arrive in Australia. She gave us enough rations to last that long, but after weeks, then months without news from us, how long could they reasonably hold on to hope?

Every single day Ba heard people share news of their friends and family who died when their boats capsized or were killed by pirates. Every day for months he heard those reports, but couldn't tell a soul about his own children. He and Mẹ grasped onto a sliver of hope that melted away a little more with every report.

My heart ached again to think of their agony and their sacrifice, knowing it took us eight months to be

155

able to send a letter to them.

~~~

During that visit, we took the very first photograph of us all together. That would have to hold our hearts steady for a while. I promised them, "We are doing our best to get you all to the United States. We already started the paperwork to sponsor you. You can live with us. We will be together again."

While we were there, we received word the sponsorship paperwork process had progressed. I used that family photograph to establish we really were a family unit, and I really had an interest in helping them.

I told my family one more time about the people we knew and the availability of housing, jobs, and food. I did have to break bad news to them: most Americans do not use fish sauce. They laughed, shook their heads, and rolled their eyes over the far-fetched idea.

We took our certified inspected videos and pictures through customs and boarded a flight back home. John remarked, "These are the poorest conditions I have ever seen, even worse than Costa Rica. But even though dirty conditions surround them, the Vietnamese people were always clean. Amazing. How do they do that?"

"Because," I explained, "they are impoverished beyond what most Americans will ever see, but their sense of honor requires that they make the best of their situation. They might have been robbed of everything else, but they cling to what they still have—their dignity."

Chapter 11

W e returned to the freedom and luxuries in the United States with an increased urgency to bring my family here with us. Those first days back here made us so thankful for the freedoms to choose our leaders, our livelihood, our home, our medical treatment, and our faith. We became even more thankful for our Capitalistic society where we could work for a fair wage, then spend it as we choose. The government did not enslave us but allowed us to live in freedom. We prayed even more fervently God would clear the path to allow them to come here.

The Immigration and Naturalization Services (INS) required numerous documents before they would approve our sponsorship application. We would have to have "all our eggs in a row." Or eggs in a basket ... or were those ducks?

We used the pictures we took in Vietnam of our complete family to help document we were indeed related and suitable sponsors. We rounded up birth certificates, documents that confirmed my citizenship, and a long list of questionnaires that produced a twelve-inch high stack of paperwork.

We brought it all to the INS, planted seeds of patience, and tried to rush them into sprouting, through what the officials reminded us would be a long process. The official shook his head in sympathy and apologized to us, saying, "It could easily take up to ten years to get everything completed from both governments." Because the two countries didn't officially communicate with each other, a Catholic agency served as mediator. A great help, but another delay. More patience required. But I fertilized those seeds with prayer every day.

~~~

In Vietnam, my sister, Thư, continued her work as a pharmacy technician and set up her own pharmacy in Saigon. She followed in the steps of our great-grandfather when she listened to customers describe their ailments and sold them an aspirin, or ibuprofen, or a vitamin to help their symptoms. Customers bought what they could afford, usually one tablet at a time when absolutely necessary, then came back the next day if they needed another.

As the other siblings graduated from high school, they had to find ways to earn some kind of living, while we waited.

And waited.

During the wait, Thư reached her twenty-first birthday. That made her technically an adult, and ineligible to be included for sponsorship under my parents' household since she aged out. We were so close and so disappointed at the same time.

~~~

We thanked our church family again for their prayers for us while we visited Vietnam, but now we asked them to pray again. This time we asked that they pray the immigration process of my family would go smoothly and quickly. They took the matter to the throne of God.

After only two years, the agency granted my parents and siblings an interview with officials about the immigration. They entered the interview room and met the American immigration official, Frank, who conducted the interview session. After the introductions and pleasantries, he picked up the documents on the desk, squared them up with a tap to the desktop, and thumbed through the papers. He called out the five names on the top of the document who were eligible for immigration with sponsorship. "This is your family?"

Ba explained to him those names were all correct, with one name missing. They were actually a family of six who had a sponsor and wanted to immigrate together, but during the time it took for all the paperwork to process, one daughter, Thư, reached her twenty-first birthday. He nodded that he understood, then frowned while they expressed their sincere desire to stay a family unit.

After their appeal, he admitted he sympathized their situation and their petition, but he was required to follow the law. Under the law Thư no longer fell under Ba's household. She represented a distinctly separate family instead. That's why her name could not be listed on the immigration application with the family.

The official could have followed the letter of the law. Legally, he should have. Instead, he issued a special waiver to include her in the family group. He scribbled out the number five and replaced it with six.

God answered our prayer from the other side of the world.

At long last, my whole immediate family now had permission to join us on American soil. "We had the green thumb to proceed!"

We also had a lot to work out before they arrived. Our eight hundred square-foot home was perfect for three, but less than ideal for a household of eleven. We emptied our savings account to make a down payment on a larger house almost three times the size of our starter home. This one had three bedrooms plus a study, and square footage that would have commanded a much larger price tag, but it happened to be next door to a chicken processing plant. That worked for us. I realized I would be "burning the midnight oil at both ends," but it would be worth every effort to have them here.

~~~

March 1994

My parents and siblings told their friends and extended family members about their move and took good-bye pictures with long-faced relatives who wished them well but still felt the sorrow of separation.

They packed all their belongings and headed south to Saigon over the same roads and ferries we traveled the previous year. Even though it seemed like the dream of their lifetime came true, the unknown, unexpected, and the possibility that something could still obstruct the plan loomed over them.

Thu knew about the great expense, the age-limit complication, and didn't want to get her hopes up she would actually be able to join us. She didn't let herself believe it could really happen even after packing and traveling, then waiting at the airport in Saigon. "It was too good to be true," she told me later.

That night they boarded a plane to join me on American soil. My family settled into their seats for the first leg of twenty-nine hours in the air. Because they left in the darkness, Thư could only see clouds out the window. She said to me later, "I might wake up in a minute and be back in my room. I can't even see land or water out the windows—it must be a dream."

After stops in Hong Kong and Japan, the stewardesses used multi-lingual cards to let them know they were about to arrive in Seattle.

Seattle, the gateway to the USA.

~~~

We worried about my family coming into the United States and making the airport connections alone without an interpreter. If there had been any way we could have made the trip with them, we would have, but we already spent our savings and were in debt for the house. John's best friend and future business partner gifted him enough miles for a round-trip ticket, so he could go to Seattle and meet my family there.

John arrived in Seattle the day before my family was to arrive, but with no money for a hotel, he slept in the airport. An INS officer struck up a conversation with him and discovered his mission to meet his Vietnamese in-laws. Of course, the INS officer knew all the ins and outs of the process and gave him a smile and said, "Come with me. I know where they will be coming in. I'll take care of them."

The plane landed safely. My weary parents and siblings passed through the same open gate to freedom

161

where I entered the United States fourteen years before. To their great relief, John's familiar face greeted them. Only then, when she saw John, did Thư believe her dream came true. She'd made it to America.

My husband is fairly tall by American standards, giant-size compared to Vietnamese. My family had met him when we visited Vietnam and realized Americans were generally taller than Vietnamese. While they took in their first view of the Seattle Airport, a basketball team passed by. My family stopped and slowly tilted their heads upward until their eyes finally reached all the way to the faces of those extraordinarily tall men. After they passed by, my wide-eyed brother asked John what they were all wondering, "Are all Americans this tall?"

John had to laugh as he shook his head and tried to assure them they were not. He helped my family navigate the next leg of their flight to Dallas-Fort Worth, then to Alabama.

I had been "up to my wall in work," preparing for their arrival. Now I had to wait these final few agonizingly long hours. I sat in the same Alabama airport where I arrived as a thirteen-year-old girl, waiting for my family finally to join me. This time I waited as the sponsor instead of a refugee. This time, my family would join me here, just as I dreamed.

As we all dreamed.

Loan, John's parents and a host of friends waited with Katherine and me. Over the last weeks, I coached my seventeen-month-old daughter how to fold her hands so she could properly greet her extended family. We waited and practiced the bow. She looked perfect in her custom-made traditional Vietnamese-style dress.

While I watched the minute hand drag around the face of my watch, I relived the joy and wonder of the first time I saw this new landscape years before. The fears of the unknown were long behind me now, but I expected my family must be experiencing the same emotions. Had they had any rice on their airplane dinner plates? I hoped my mother remembered I promised to have rice and fish sauce.

Before we came to the airport, I made sure the "spic and spanky" house had everything ready for them, but still reviewed my plans to acquaint them with the house, and checked the food and linen lists in my head one more time. Everything had to be perfect. I had as many things as I could in place, to make this monumental transition as easy as possible, and now at eight-months pregnant with our son, my chore list had to be accomplished sooner rather than later.

The sluggish hands on the clock finally reached the scheduled time of arrival and their plane landed. John escorted them to the area where I waited. When I saw them, I lifted Katherine up out of her seat, smoothed her dress, pointed at her maternal grandparents moving toward her, and Katherine bowed perfectly for everyone, stealing their hearts.

Finally, one by one, I embraced each family member on American soil. My parents took me by the shoulders and looked down, smiling to see the evidence of their grandson growing inside me. So many prayers were answered that day, in that moment.

Our good friends who came to share in our day of joy, waited to the side to give us room to greet family, then eased in to join the noisy crowd. They shook hands, smiled, nodded, and tried to explain their connection to me and their happiness to welcome them here. Their welcome and support needed no translation.

Between the excitement and anxiety, none of them had slept on the plane. So, we gathered the tired travelers and transported them to our house, their new home. Loan moved out of our aunt and uncle's home to move in with us and be with her immediate family again while she finished her college degree. So we went from a household of three with one more on the way, to a household of ten, soon to be eleven.

That first night I had the great honor of doing what Loan and I dreamed about over the years. I showed my family around their new American home. The four sisters shared one bedroom furnished with bunk beds and a mattress on the floor. My brother slept in the sunroom. My parents slept in the study. John and I had one bedroom and our daughter had one bedroom she shared with her brother when he arrived a few weeks later. The eleven of us shared two bathrooms, one upstairs and one down.

My mother enjoyed her shower that night but didn't realize the shower curtain needed to go to the inside of the tub, resulting in a minor flood in the upstairs bathroom.

The day couldn't have been more perfect. I had fulfilled my dream. After years of plans and prayers, my whole family slept under my roof and under the banner of freedom that night.

No longer a dream, we were together.

In the United States of America.

I doubt God revealed to John those many years ago when he married this Asian woman, he would also inherit her whole family. But he not only loved me, he loved them, and welcomed them—all of them—into our home. "He is one of a million."

Western culture traditionally serves certain foods for breakfast including bacon and eggs—and biscuits here in the South, and on special occasions, sweets like pancakes and waffles. John decided to honor our guests' first morning in the Land of Opportunity with an official "Welcome to the USA Breakfast." My sweet husband proudly prepared his homemade waffles to give them a taste of an American specialty.

When they woke and gathered for breakfast, my family members politely took a bite and tried not to choke. They exchanged baffled looks and managed to swallow. Then as nicely as possible, they asked if we had some leftover rice and maybe some soy sauce they could eat instead.

Vietnamese cuisine rarely includes sweets, and certainly never as the main dish. Not only that, our menus were never specific to a time of day. We enjoyed rice and some savory topping for nearly every meal, so this sweet deliciousness Americans considered a wonderful treat, did not appeal to their Vietnamese palates at all. I believe "repulsed" would be the best translation for their description. My sweet American husband; "he is one in a dozen."

Although they believed the impressive box in the kitchen to be some sort of a computer, we introduced them to the joy of microwaving food. They followed us around the kitchen eager to learn about the stove and oven and refrigerator. As long as they had rice, soy sauce, and Ramen Noodles, they were fine. I even pulled out a bottle of fish sauce to welcome them. They were tired, a little overwhelmed, but happy.

Because their flight arrived after dark, Thu wondered why there were so few lights and where the neighbors could be as we drove to our house. She didn't see what her new home looked like until the following morning. In the daylight, she could see outside that our neighborhood had individual homes laid out far more spaciously than the townhouse-type style of our hometown. In comparison, she thought we were practically alone, especially with the quietness of closed windows.

~~~

At church the following Sunday, John thanked the congregation for their prayers and told them my family arrived safely. The whole family. Never underestimate the power of God's people praying, and His ability to answer every single prayer. We continued our normal routine and included the family in it to help them learn how to navigate the city and the basics of life here.

With great joy, I introduced my parents to an American grocery store. I followed them up and down the aisles while they explored the canned and fresh items. My father picked up everything to see the country of origin. If "made in China" appeared on the label, he grunted, shook his head, and put it back on the shelf. I remembered my own amazement those years ago at this wonderful place filled with more food than I had seen in my lifetime, and considered it an honor to share this abundance with them.

We gradually introduced them to some American cuisine they found palatable. We easily converted them to the joys of pizza and spaghetti. Mẹ effortlessly learned to cook on a grill. John, my hunter, supplied fish for her to grill. American John automatically cut off the heads and discarded the bones. After considerable—shall we say "discussion"—Mẹ finally agreed to toss the fish heads. It took far more discussion before she threw out the bones. Back home, nothing would be wasted, certainly not the tender, juicy heads.

When John went squirrel hunting that season and brought back his bounty, my mother gladly filleted and grilled them. After their first taste-test, my family decided squirrel tasted a lot like mouse.

Thu admitted a little homesickness hit her those first weeks, partly because she didn't know what to do, where to go, or how to communicate when she went somewhere. We made a point to drive the family around town so they could become familiar with the city and its opportunities for work and fun.

The fast food restaurants seemed to be a good starting point. Thu got to use some of the English she learned in Vietnam and earned her first American paycheck at McDonald's. This gave her the confidence she could make a living here and would be okay. Of course, I remembered and sympathized with all those emotions and reminded her I would help her any way I could.

We shuttled them back and forth to job interviews and helped with translating questions and answers while they enrolled in English as second language (ESL) classes. Then, as they became familiar with the city and the language, some began college. We fell into a routine in the use of the house, bathrooms, mealtimes, laundry, and everything that goes with that many adults living under the same roof.

Ba began a job at the chicken processing plant next to our house and walked to work until he saved enough to buy a car and got his driver's license.

I savored every precious moment with Mẹ. At the birth of my daughter, we were a world apart. Now she pampered me, showered me with motherly advice, and held my hand at the birth of our son, John Boyer, III. To eliminate confusion over John my husband, John my father-in-law, and John our son, we called him J.B. She took on the responsibilities of helping me with duties of meal preparation and taking care of my two young children.

Her eyes lit up when I introduced her to the local store that stocked plenty of fish sauce. Thankful to finally be reunited, she told me, "We knew we wanted to give our children the best opportunities we could, but when the war came ... well, we only had enough to send you two. We knew the others would probably never get to go, but at least we could send two."

"I am so glad you did, and that we are here together now."

~~~

1995

After the excitement of the previous year, we treated ourselves to a trip to the beautiful Gulf Coast. The eleven of us found a way to fit into our Mercury seven-passenger van. John drove and I sat in the front passenger seat. We strapped our two children in car seats in the very back, removed the middle seats in between the front and back, which left enough room for the rest of the family to sit on the floorboard.

To pass the time, someone brought a Chinese card game and they used real currency to keep up with points. Some of my sisters found clipping plastic butterfly hair clips, meant for our little girl, to John's hair while he drove to be far more entertaining. The more John ignored them, the more clips they added.

By the time his hair had more clips than hair showing, blue lights flashed behind us. John pulled out his driver license and placed both hands on the steering wheel, balancing the license between two fingers, and rolled down the window.

The small-town policeman sauntered up to the window, and from behind heavily mirrored aviator sunglasses, questioned John, "Driver license?"

"Yes, sir." John carefully handed it over.

"Where ya' goin', son?"

"To the beach, sir."

"Do you know how fast you were going?"

"No, sir."

While he quizzed John, the officer leaned his head through the window and saw John's baby-clipped hair and our group of Vietnamese people on the floor of the van with cards and cash, and either decided we posed only a low-level threat to the community, or else he pitied John. Maybe both.

He handed John his license and warned him to, "Slow down, son," then sighed with a shake of his head. "You have a good day."

"Thank you, sir. Thank you."

When he was out of earshot, we roared in laughter to think of the story the officer had to tell. "You won't believe what I saw today ..."

~~~

When my children were older, Mẹ took a job outside the home for a time. Once wealthy business owners, now both parents proudly worked to debone chicken for

American minimum wage. They earned the equivalent of several annual salaries in Vietnam in a couple of months and never took the great privilege and responsibility of earning a living for granted.

Loan lived with us for a couple of years until she finished college. With her EE degree in hand, she landed a job and rented a home of her own. When she moved out, Ba and Mẹ and my siblings went to live with her, leaving John and me and our little family of four.

Thu became friends with another Vietnamese lady who lived in our area and visited church with her. She told me of the profound sense of peace there. We'd missed so many sister-talks in the last fifteen years, it gave me great joy to be a part of her journey from "feeling peace" to learning how to talk with God herself.

I watched her grow in her knowledge of God and into an avid prayer warrior. She began to understand He had a plan for her life and daily prayed He would guide her within that plan. God used her tender heart to work with a Catholic orphanage in Vietnam, where children born with any deformity or disability were sent to the orphanage rather than "bring a curse on their family." The Catholic church had assisted in their immigration and in mine, and in honor of how they helped her family, she continues to help raise money for those *Abandoned Little Angels*.

~~~

I enjoyed a wonderful life with my family here on the same soil with my wonderful husband and our two wonderful children. While they were in school, I helped in every way I could, from PTA fund-raising chairman to working with the Band Parents' Association.

I enjoyed a wonderful time of growing my faith in God who had so wonderfully provided for me. I enjoyed a wonderful time of sharing my faith with my family and seeing several come to belief in the one true God.

Won-der-full.

During all this wonderfulness, we moved our church membership to a church closer to our home with more programs for our children. The pastor and several church members even lived in our neighborhood.

But through a series of hurtful events, the friendship between our family and church members did not survive. The enemy laid a trap for us, we fell for it, and faded out of that church and settled into a routine without a church family. We even homeschooled our children for a couple of years to isolate ourselves from wounds inflicted from the situation.

God nudged us to remove ourselves even further, and we relocated to a nearby city. There we visited a couple of churches, but felt like we didn't fit in.

One year passed into another year and another and another, without setting our feet inside a church. We became accustomed to life without a church family. We had a good family income and believed we didn't need the drama and hurt from church people. We really didn't even need God anymore. I liked being in charge of my life, in "the driver's seat" so to speak. Self-sufficiency worked for us. I was completely "condensed of it." Or should I say, "convinced." We didn't realize that Satan had led us down a "wild goose trail."

I filled the void with plenty of volunteer work. The Salvation Army had helped us, and I repaid some of the kindness shown to me. I worked with the county Angel Tree program for several years. I also delivered meals for Meals On Wheels. I worked with Kids To Love that helps children in foster care. I served as a Vietnamese translator for AshaKiran, an agency that provides services to people in dangerous situations. My heart went out to the Abandoned Little Angels orphanage in Vietnam. I became more involved in raising money for them and made several trips to Vietnam to deliver the money in person to the nuns there.

Even though we substituted good works for church for almost a decade, God never gave up on us. Some dear friends kept praying God would lead us back to church. He heard those prayers and kept tugging at our hearts.

John and I both realized we missed being with other Christians and worshipping God in a church setting. Our son, J.B., told us he wanted to start reading the Bible that had long sat unopened on his bedside table. Katherine told us she no longer believed God existed. She turned away from God as we had.

That brought us back into the reality of how much we did need God. He used our children to motivate us to do more than realize we needed Him. We also realized we needed to get back in right standing with Him and return to church—for our sakes and the sake of our children. Like a veil removed from our eyes, we could now clearly see we needed His help to mend the broken parts of our family. Finally seeking Him again, we found Him already there. God picked up our pieces and helped us return to our real mission: to serve Him.

He led us to Christian counselors who ministered to us and prayed for us and with us. There, we heard the truths that healed our hearts, deeply scarred from our previous hurt. We visited the church where those counselors attended and found our new church home and family.

God used each sermon to speak directly to me about my need for a closer relationship with Him. The Holy Spirit ministered to our brokenness every week. My heart cried in pain to realize He rescued and saved me for a purpose, yet I spent so many years without pursuing what He wanted for me. I selfishly kept my life in my hands doing what I wanted, when I should have been listening to, obeying, and serving Him.

My heart rejoiced as we made new friends in the faith. We joined together with a small group of couples about our age and circumstance, and we met weekly outside church in each other's homes. John and I already learned that trying to get by alone only gave us an excuse to distance ourselves from God, so this group became good accountability partners.

We flourished within this Christian fellowship. More than fellowship, it became a place where we shared life together. We started by serving dessert, then served one another by praying with and for each other. Fed with dessert and the Holy Spirit, we dug into the Bible. The more we gathered together and studied God's Word, the more we found out that we shared many of the same struggles.

We had no idea these other couples experienced some of the same struggles and worries we had when we saw them at Sunday school and church. We all tended to hide our difficulties and present a façade of "we have it all together" while we were there. But in the safety of our small group, we admitted that we were all vulnerable, all sinners and needed accountability and truth to stay on the right path. The hurdles became far easier to navigate with a group who cared about us and prayed over us and sought the will of God in every aspect of the situation. We prayed and pointed each other to God, no matter what.

With this close-knit group, we found a depth of Christian friendship like none other we'd ever experienced. This friendship/fellowship and accountability to stick with God's Word and one another motivated us to rekindle our desire to learn more about the character of God and our relationship to Him. We dug into His Word and relished everything we could learn about Him.

We called it a "life group" because we are walking through life together, with God leading our path. We truly became the "2 a.m. friends"—the kind you could call in the middle of the night and know they would be there for you. We were there for each other "365 days a week," or something like that.

After a time of building ourselves in the Word of God, we shifted from thoughts of helping to build up each other in our faith to helping others outside our group. We realized we had a built-in ministering opportunity to reach more than our little group. This small cell of believers grew from the five original couples to include four more couples.

Our expectation and our prayer is God will branch us out even more and start more small groups that will give birth to more groups. God has changed our desires from doing what we like—even doing good things—to serving Him first and foremost, an amazing transformation from one who completely ignored God, to one who relies on Him day by day.

God has been teaching me about reconciliation and has challenged me to pray for the Malaysian people. Not a one-time prayer, but to pray for them for this entire year. Yes, I now pray for the people who tried to kill me. I pray they will come to know Him. God showed mercy to me; now I can show mercy to others and do it without reservation.

~~~

2016

Penny, a tennis partner, belonged to the local DAR group and invited me to tell about my escape from the grips of Communism and about my life now in this land of freedom. I gladly shared with them my experiences and my love for this country where I can work toward a dream unshackled by the government. We all proudly waved Old Glory and reveled in our freedoms and opportunities.

Without telling me what they were doing, that local chapter gathered letters from those who knew me, my story, my work with various charities, and used those letters to support my nomination for the DAR Americanism Award. The state headquarters chose me as the state winner and submitted it for the national honor.

Penny called me one day with unexpected news. Out of all the local and state nominations from around the country, they chose me to receive the national DAR Americanism Award—for leadership, trustworthiness, patriotism and service—the highest honor a naturalized citizen could receive from the DAR.

At a lovely ceremony in May 2016, they presented

me with a beautiful DAR medal and certificate along with the letters of recommendation they collected from church friends, the mayor, Salvation Army, and Abandoned Little Angels.

I felt it my duty to give back to this nation that has given me so much. Honored and humbled at this recognition, I could only praise God for all He has done for me, and renewed my allegiance to Him and this great country.

Chapter 12

Later in 2016, John's brother developed health issues and was hospitalized. The doctors determined he needed triple bypass surgery. The family gathered at the hospital.

After a long day of waiting together during the surgery, doctors delivered us news of good results for my brother-in-law. The next day, as he began to stabilize, we rotated in and out of the hospital, taking turns to go home and get some rest.

It was John's turn to rest at home, while I stayed at the hospital. I don't remember if I ate much that day, but I felt strange—tingly—I was losing my ability to focus. I turned to the lady standing next to me in the ICU waiting room, tapped her on the shoulder and said, "I don't feel good."

Just after the words came out of my mouth, my body stiffened and I lost consciousness. Afraid I would topple over, several adults pushed hard against me to press me down into a chair.

Meanwhile, John had settled into a couch in his

office at home and fell asleep. He dreamed he saw me being pressed, crushed, and hurting. Waking up, he quickly reached for his phone to call and check on me. When he picked it up, he found a text from our sister-in-law, Leslie. "Get to the hospital. Something is wrong with Thanh."

While the doctors tried to determine what happened to me, the logical first thought was that I fainted from fatigue or perhaps from not eating well. I woke up with a slight headache, thought it might have been an episode of low blood sugar, and dismissed it as that. Frankly, if it had happened while I was alone at home, I would have never mentioned it.

When John arrived, the doctors agreed that my blood sugar probably bottomed out, which caused me to faint. They reasoned that I just needed to eat, then I would be okay to go home. Almighty God already knew what happened in me. He placed someone in the waiting room with me who recognized exactly what happened, and she made a point to speak to John. She informed him that she personally knew seizures and firmly told him what she saw me go through was more than a fainting spell. She had witnessed me seizing.

John reported back to the doctor about the first-hand witness who believed I experienced a seizure, and the doctor ordered a CAT scan to be safe. The scan revealed something we never expected, a tumor. Yes, I had headaches for years, but thought they were sinus headaches or maybe allergies. Besides, we were there to support John's brother, not confront our own medical crisis. *What was happening?*

My mind switched back to a few years before when my aunt, who came to the United States with me, also had a brain tumor. Hers was deep, which made for a difficult surgery. During her operation, they nicked a blood vessel and the bleeding from it could not be contained, throwing her into a life-threatening situation. After all the attempts to save her life were exhausted, they placed her on life-support machines.

Instead of waking, she made no progress at all.

They waited.

The doctors and family watched her vital signs, stable, but saw no progress.

They waited.

They studied every blood test, every physical test, every brain scan, but found no activity.

She was gone.

There was no point in waiting any longer. The family made the heart-wrenching decision to remove her from life-support equipment.

With the machines that kept her body alive turned off, her body should have shut down.

But God had a different plan.

Instead of her body shutting down, it turned on. Beyond anyone's expectation, she moved a finger. No one could dismiss that she was still there. She regained consciousness, and after rehabilitation, recovered most of her former abilities other than residual blindness in one eye, and loss of short-term memory.

I pushed aside the memory of her brain surgery experience to focus on what the doctor had to say about my CAT scan. I might not even need surgery. He put some images on a screen and pointed out a ping pong-sized mass near the base of my brain, and how it pressed on blood vessels that needed to feed my brain. He wanted to consult with the radiologist before we discussed options and prognosis.

He left our room, and John and I waited together. With this time alone, John relayed to me about the dream that awoke him that let him know I was in danger. That dream affirmed to us both that God was at work, so neither of us panicked or even worried. The peace of God which surpasses all understanding (Philippians 4:7) flooded over both of us, despite the replays in our minds of my aunt's experience.

When the doctors finally knocked on the door of my room, they gave us the good news—they believed the mass was most likely benign.

The bad news followed closely behind. The restricted blood flow to my brain already had caused some blood vessels to shut off. Some had rerouted in an effort to supply my brain with blood, but I needed to see a neurosurgeon promptly.

We scheduled an appointment and met with the surgeon. Our first question—could we just watch it for a while rather than go directly to a surgical intervention?

He drew his eyebrows together, pursed his lips, and shook his head, as a quick dismissal of that idea. There were no other options. A tumor this size, already pressing on the blood supply could not be ignored. A growing tumor would mean more seizure activity, and could create more permanent problems with my sight and balance. "If you were eighty years old, I would recommend you leave it alone. But it is not worth the risk at your age."

We both took deep breaths and peered at each other, then nodded in agreement to the doctor's opinion for surgical intervention. Peace continued to prevail as the surgeon talked with us about what to expect with brain surgery. He mentioned possible complications like my aunt experienced but assured us those were rare.

By that time, the overwhelming peace of God didn't allow me to entertain any fear whatsoever about the situation, no matter the outcome. Because I knew God was in it, I hoped that He might use this to minister to family members who were not living according to the will of God at that time. I earnestly prayed that God might use this to encourage some remaining family members, to seek Him, trust Him, and accept Him as their Savior.

Because my family already experienced sending a loved one off to surgery to remove a brain tumor, when I called them together to tell them about mine, I tried to break it to them as gently as I could. The news sucked every molecule of oxygen out of the room. Everyone froze in place and silently processed my situation. No doubt they replayed their memories of my aunt's experience. Their anxiety was clear, even behind brave faces.

On the day of surgery, they gathered around me in the hospital room to take a photograph of us all together, perhaps for the last time.

I was ready.

They were not.

I had many talks with God leading up to this day. Long ago I surrendered my heart and life to Him. I made the mistake of withdrawing from Him for far too long before, and I would not withhold anything from Him now. If I didn't walk out of the hospital, I would walk straight into His arms.

I offered one final prayer after they wheeled me away from my family. Before I reached the operating room, I reminded myself and God that He could use my life or death any way He wished. "If this is Your plan to soften a heart that needs to come to You, then I am okay with that."

God as always knew my heart and heard my prayer. He answered, "No, you have to wake up. John needs you." That is the last thing I remember before I slipped under the anesthesia and into unconsciousness—safe in His strong and mighty hand, and firmly rooted in His perfect peace.

In the surgical waiting room, my husband and children waited with my parents, siblings, in-laws, life group family from church, tennis friends, and my two best friends, Pam and Lynne, to wait for news. They all wrote their well-wishes and prayers for me in a book while they waited.

Thu was anxious, knowing what had happened with our aunt. She and I had been apart for so many years, and now we enjoyed our lives together again as a family, and had grown into sisters in faith as well. She sat with Pam, who was also a Christian. Together, Thu and Pam fervently prayed that God would "make everything good for Thanh." He did, and He also granted her peace and calm.

When someone called out for the family of "Boyer," all heads popped up, eager to hear any news. They held their collective breath while John sprinted over to hear what the surgeon had to say. He returned to my family and repeated the doctor's prognosis. "Everything looked good," and two people at a time would be able to visit me in the ICU soon.

Everyone exhaled in unison and smiled in relief. Finally able to breathe, my family realized they were hungry. Thu went to buy some takeout for the family.

~~~

The surgery required that the surgeon cut through the muscle and skull to remove the tumor. The muscles were reattached, but the surgeon didn't replace the base of my skull. By leaving soft tissue in place of the bone, he hoped it would allow room for swelling and hopefully avoid the need for a second surgery if swelling became an issue. In his experience, those muscles and ligaments should grow back strongly enough to take the place of the bone he removed.

So, they rolled me out of surgery minus a tumor and part of my skull, severed neck muscles, and only about half of my long black Asian hair. I traded all that for a fancy white bandage around my head that looked a lot like a turban.

When I roused from anesthesia enough to open my eyes, John and Katherine were looking at me and my turban from under furrowed brows.

John called out the usual battery of tests, "Can you see me? Do you know who I am? How many fingers do you see?"

I tried to dismiss him and closed my eyes to suppress the excruciating pain.

A nurse opened up the morphine drip to flow more freely into my veins, but that pain relief came at a high cost. A loathsome side-effect took the place of the pain. Retching with nausea and dry heaves was not welcome on a good day, much less with a semi-severed head.

The doctors decided to reduce my morphine to take away some of the nausea. Otherwise I might pull loose some of their delicate embroidery stitches on the back of my head. It did reduce the nausea, but left me in agony. I felt at least "six feet under the weather," or however that goes. I only knew "if I had been a horse, I would have shot myself."

John comforted me the best he could. He told me that the whole family was there for me, waiting in the waiting room, hoping to see me.

Every muscle I moved caused more pain—breathing, talking, and opening my eyelids. I managed to swallow, then firmly whispered through clenched teeth, "Send them home."

By then, Thu had returned with food for everyone. John came out to give them the details. When they asked to see me, he tried to lighten the mood by telling them I was so bossy I demanded everyone go home.

They read between the lines, understood, and left.

By the grace and mercy of God, I survived the surgery and the pain. Three days later they discharged me and sent me home to recuperate. I rested that night at home without monitors, IV's, or alarms.

The following day I wanted to shower. Next to being home, showering in my own bathroom ranked pretty high on my to-do list. Even though I didn't really feel like it, I stubbornly thought I could force my body to do its bidding, and I wanted a shower. Like it or not, there are some things over which I have no control. I received that newsflash about the time my body failed me. I had just enough time to call out to John, "I don't feel good" before I completely passed out in his arms.

God had always protected me and provided for me in every situation, even before I knew Him. He didn't fail me this time either. A trip to the hospital scrambled the doctors into action with the fear that I was bleeding from surgery. An emergency MRI revealed that I had no internal hemorrhage. The doctors believed I was weak from surgery and declared it safe for me to return home. I just had to take it easy. Believe me, I got the message that time.

John once again drove me, exhausted and suffering, back to our home. Home is a wonderful place. The best place. Even in times of intense suffering.

~~~

If anyone squeezed me, a pill was going to pop out, so I searched for other ways to cope with the pain. Even the weight from my lopsided haircut pulled against the raw muscles and they screamed in protest. The poor muscles and ligaments were doing all they could to try to grow back, support my head on my neck, and keep my brain from slipping out where the skull was removed. The severed muscles were in no mood to do more, and I was in no mood to deal with more pain than necessary. So, off came the remaining hair. Now, with one less battle to fight, I managed to keep my head upright with a little less struggle, a little less pain. One small victory.

I found that propped "upright," the severed muscles could rest. So, I sat and slept with my head elevated for the next six months in a chair or on the couch until I was finally able to sleep in my own bed again.

With days spent homebound, alone and healing, the busyness of life gave way to spending time with God. The more time I spent with Him, the more I realized how precious He is to me and how precious I am to

Him.

Before the brain tumor entered my life, I filled my days with things that I thought had great importance. "I had been up to my wall in work." I planned and prepared our family meals, household duties, and our business. I served on committees, worked at fundraisers, and played with the tennis club.

After the surgery, I could do none of those things. I couldn't even focus my eyes to watch television or read or bear the noise of the television or the radio playing softly in the background.

God slowed me down enough so that I could take a step back and see that I had already done what I promised I would never do again. I placed Him in the passenger seat. I spent far too much time trying to be in control, worrying about and fretting over things I didn't understand and couldn't possibly change. "I kept running into that brick road."

With no pressing meetings or household activities on my calendar, I sat in the presence of God and heard Him speak of His love for me. I handed over control of all my former responsibilities to others and gave my complete attention to God. My days now filled with listening to Him, I began to rest in Him, and trust Him even more. I traded my pride in all my hard work for time with Him to work on my heart.

With no distractions, God and I wandered together back to those early years of my life. He reminded me that His hand was there with me before I even knew Him. From the Communist official who didn't report my family, to the storm that hurried the pirates away, to the shot that cured the dysentery, to His preparing my husband for me on this side of the planet. The more I remembered how much He already did for me, the more I trusted Him to continue loving me.

I fell even more deeply in love with my precious Savior and realized all the time I spent worrying revealed my lack of faith in Him. I thought I needed to be in control of all those things. He got through to me that I didn't need to worry about having everything under control because He already did.

Those first weeks brought extraordinary pain and extravagant peace. My pain subsided a tiny bit every week, and my faith grew stronger every day.

~~~

After the initial risk of infection diminished, the doctors allowed visitors to spend time with me. My wonderful friends and family reached out to help me in every way. They brought food, offered back massages, house cleaning—anything they could think of. They were fantastic.

I can tell you that tumors solve a lot of problems. Want meals delivered? Get a brain tumor. Need a back massage? If you have great friends and family, just get a tumor. They will show up.

Everyone noticed my short hair and bandages, but my church family and Christian members of my birth family also noticed something else in me. After talking with me, they remarked that it was evident that God had an even greater hold on me than they ever saw in me before. I was in a situation over which I had no control, and on the sideline from my active lifestyle, yet I was not frustrated or discouraged.

They set down their casseroles, and we talked about the serious possible outcomes of this tumor and surgery. It could still bring drastic changes or even

187

bring an end to my life. I fully realized all those possibilities but had no concern or anxiety about any of them.

I explained to each of them that it wasn't that I was particularly strong or brave; I just released my worries to Almighty God. His strength filled me with a great measure of peace no matter the outcome. They smiled, listened, and became witnesses to my genuine lack of fear. They saw firsthand the peace of God that so completely filled me and changed me. The more we talked and shared, the more my family and friends were inspired to grow in that same source of strength and courage. God used my tumor time to share a treasured blessing, not to mention some delicious casseroles.

As the weeks passed, I began to heal and regain strength, but before I could drive a car by myself, I had to be seizure-free for at least six months. My friends worked up a spreadsheet with blocks of times every day, and they each signed up to drive me places several times a week. "I was back on the shopping block."

~~~

Because my aunt and I both developed tumors in our brains, my siblings each decided to be scanned for similar brain tumors. The doctors didn't believe it to be an inherited tendency, but we were all exposed to the aftereffects of bombs and other chemicals in the war zone we once called home. So, one by one they were each tested.

My sister Loan and I already discussed how remote the chances must be for more than one of us to have a brain tumor, but she went in for her scan anyway. By the time she was about to go in, she became a little nervous. The technician recognized her anxiety and asked if she would like to hear music during the MRI.

"Is there a Christian station available?"

The technician smiled. "I'll play something for you."

The song he chose was one she had heard frequently on her favorite Christian radio station. God calmed her mind in the MRI tunnel, with words from a song she already knew and that had great meaning for her. She texted me after the test. *Whatever He decides will be okay. I feel a great peace and His presence with me.* Loan's results were completely clear. No tumors.

When it was time for Thu's MRI, she prayed, *God, I know you are always with me. I don't know Your plan, but I know You are with me. As long as You are close, I will not be afraid.*

Her MRI revealed a tumor embedded within her brain in a different location than mine, but deeper. God granted her such a complete peace that she didn't even tell us about the findings until after she made all the arrangements for surgery.

While I would never wish anyone else to go through this, especially someone I love, I also believed it was a precious gift to be able to walk the road with my younger sister, knowing I had already traveled it safely before her.

Only about three months after my operation, my family once again gathered around a family member about to undergo brain surgery. We held hands, prayed, and watched her be wheeled away.

We continued to pray in the waiting room and had friends all over town joining our prayers. The surgeon reported to us that the tumor did not appear to be malignant and had probably been growing there a number of years, even as much as a decade. They believed the surgery was successful and she would recover well without any complications or residual effects.

As soon as they allowed visitors, I tiptoed into the room, sat at the bedside of my turbaned little sister, and picked up her cool limp hand. She squeezed it slightly and opened her eyes. Immediately I recognized the pain on her face.

I looked up and asked the nurse about her pain medication.

"It has to be approved by the doctor first."

"She just had brain surgery and the doctor hasn't already prescribed pain management medications?"

She shook her head, "No."

I looked back at my little sister, took in a deep breath, and grasped her hand with both of mine. "The enforcer" had to call for help. I drew near to her face and stared into those pleading eyes and said, "We have to pray."

We prayed confidently and diligently that God would take her pain away, or make her pass out, do something to spare her from the extreme pain until the doctor approved some medicine. *God, please let it be the right kind of drug for her to help her through this and help her not to be sick. Please give her peace and calm.*

Ba saw her extreme pain from where he stood beyond the bed. This parent who did everything he could possibly do to help his children had to stand by helplessly as she suffered. He couldn't bring himself to come any nearer to his daughter's grimaced face, so he waited quietly at a distance. A silent witness, willing to do anything, but unable.

After we prayed, Thu realized others were in the room, forced her eyes open, and looked at each person. Putting her horrid pain aside, she made eye contact with each one and called out their name, so they would know she could see and recognize them. Maybe that would give them some assurance that she really was okay. If she could do nothing for her own pain, at least she could ease their pain a little.

She confided in me that she'd already prayed as I had, that if God could use this to bring some family member to know Him, she would consider this to be a good thing. Maybe our parents and remaining unsaved siblings might see that she was not worried, and it might help them realize they need God too.

My sister by birth and my sister in Christ, with our pixie haircuts and zipper-style staple scars, proudly call ourselves the "Tumor Twins." We missed many years of growing up together, but we had the great blessing of walking the recovery road together.

The Next Step

My tumor twin and I and other family members now live without fear. Not just from medical issues that tried to take our lives, but from Socialism/Communism that tried to take our ability to think, work, and worship. It required sacrifice and endurance, but my family eventually reunited under the banner of freedom. The hardships that overwhelmed me at the time proved to be worth the pain, the suffering, the tremendous cost. We have thrived.

Although far outside my comfort zone, I speak about my experiences with small groups, extending my gratitude to all those who helped me each step of the way—God, my parents, sponsors, husband, siblings, friends, and the US military personnel who fought on my behalf.

Over the last several years, God and my friends have prompted me to compile these events in a book. While I wanted to be obedient to whatever God called me to do, I told Him frankly that I "could not do that." If He wanted me to write a book, He needed to send me an author.

Meanwhile, a friend shared a book written by a local author. As I read the first page, I realized this might be the writer I asked God to send. I called her. We met. She also wanted to be obedient to God and had prayed He would direct her to her next writing project. We prayed together, and got started on this book. Just like that, God answered two prayers at once.

So, the purpose of this book is more than just retelling the amazing events of my life. I hope that if you are in a circumstance that seems devastating, it will cause you to remember to **hold on**—even when sharks circle around you. God may be working something wonderful that you will only see after you are on dry ground.

When I look back at how He brought me through more than most people experience in a lifetime, I know I can **trust Him** to lead me forward from here, no matter the direction He takes me. He is worthy of your trust too.

I also hope you realize the great value of the freedoms of our republic and how quickly that liberty can vanish. Look past the empty promises, and **stand firm for freedom,** even if it comes at great sacrifice and cost.

When you see a **Vietnam veteran**, please tell them you know of at least one little girl who is extremely thankful for their help when Communism steamrolled across her land. Tell them of my deep gratitude for their efforts to help my family during the darkest days of our lives. You might even express your own appreciation for those who serve to protect our country from similar threats today.

If you don't already, please find a place to **wave Old Glory**. That banner of freedom represents a great treasure we should never take for granted. Because I lived in a country where my freedoms vanished with the stroke of a pen, perhaps I treasure it more than most.

In 1777, the Continental Congress passed a resolution "that the flag of the thirteen United States be thirteen stripes, alternate red and white; that the union be thirteen stars, white in a blue field, representing a new constellation."[viii] From a book about the flag published in 1977 by the House of Representatives, "Those stars are a symbol of the heavens and the divine goal to which man has aspired from time immemorial; the stripe is symbolic of the rays of light emanating from the sun."

Charles Thompson, Secretary of the Continental Congress, reporting to Congress on the Great Seal, stated, "The colors of the pales (the vertical stripes) are those used in the flag of the United States of America; White signifies purity and innocence, Red, hardiness & valour [sic], and Blue, the color of the Chief (the broad band above the stripes) signifies vigilance, perseverance & justice."[ix]

During the war of 1812, the British captured Washington D.C., and soon after, their warships bombarded Fort McHenry for a solid twenty-five hours. Some bombshells exploded early, leaving red flares across the sky.

Although the British specifically targeted the flag flying over the fort, the valiant men defending it used their bodies to keep the flagpole up—even though it exposed them personally to the bombs and gunfire.

194

When one man fell, another quickly came to hold the standard. Over and over through the night, valiant soldiers stepped up and gave their last ounce of life to protect the banner of freedom.

Through the night Francis Scott Key, known as a man of prayer, caught glimpses of the flag as bombs lit the night sky. How long could they hold out? If the British took Fort McHenry, would they have the upper hand? Did our soldiers have the measure of sacrifice, valor, and perseverance necessary to protect our freedom? Would a divine intervention take place?

When dawn's light revealed Old Glory tattered, but still waving over the fort, Francis Scott Key penned the poem we have adopted as our national anthem. The inspiring first and fourth verses:

O say can you see, by the dawn's early light What so proudly we hail'd at the twilight's last gleaming, Whose broad stripes and bright stars through the perilous fight O'er the ramparts we watch'd were so gallantly streaming?
And the rocket's red glare, the bomb bursting in air, Gave proof through the night that our flag was still there, O say does that star-spangled banner yet wave O'er the land of the free and the home of the brave?

~~

O thus be it ever when freemen shall stand Between their lov'd home and the war's desolation! Blest with vict'ry and peace may the heav'n rescued land Praise the power that hath made and preserv'd us a nation!
Then conquer we must, when our cause it is just, And this be our motto – "In God is our trust," And the

195

Thanh Duong Boyer with Lisa Worthey Smith

*star-spangled banner in triumph shall wave O'er the
land of the free and the home of the brave.*

Epilogue

My paternal grandparents

Liêm Dương (Ông Nôi), my paternal grandfather. One of the wealthiest men in the county, whose name on a local hospital spoke of his generosity to the town, died in 1977 after losing his land, homes, and businesses.

My paternal grandmother, Ba Nôi, managed to survive in Vietnam. She died in 2004.

My maternal grandparents

Ông Ngoai, my maternal grandfather, died in Vietnam, within months after my paternal grandfather died.

Ba Ngoai, my maternal grandmother, continued the fish sauce business, and died after 2000.

My parents

My Tân Dương, my father (Ba). Ba's mother gave him the name, My, at birth, which means "American." Later they gave him the name Tân, though most of his relatives still use the name, My.

He and my mother (Mẹ) allowed the Communist

197

official and his family to stay in their home even after he was not required to do so. Ba knew they could not afford a place of their own. The official realized we did not come home from our "visit with relatives," and told Ba he knew what was going on, but would not report them.

Although he spoke Chinese, Cambodian, French, Vietnamese, and English, and was an astute businessman, after coming to the US, Ba gladly worked for minimum wage at a Sweet Sue chicken-processing plant deboning chicken for years. Ba and Mẹ both retired from there with numerous awards for their excellent work. Both are now American citizens. They spend a couple of months in Vietnam every year visiting friends and relatives.

Their children – All American citizens.

Thanh. I lead a coffee-talk on Fridays. There we share our concerns and pray for each other. John and I are active in church and in small-group Bible studies, volunteer with various ministries, and help support an orphanage in Vietnam. We are praying about some new mission opportunities on college campuses to help students retain their identities in Christ.

We suspect the brain tumor might have been caused from exposure to Agent Orange or chemicals from nearby bombs.

Both of our children are blessings from God, and we pray every day that they always pursue His purpose for their lives.

Katherine, our daughter. Her Vietnamese relatives gave her the name Thao [Ta-o], which means "respectful to parents." She is currently in medical school.

John Boyer, III ("J.B."), our son. His Vietnamese relatives gave him the name Thien [Te-in] which means, "wise." He works as an electrical engineer in Alabama.

Loan. My sister married and has children. She works as an electrical engineer in Alabama.

Thu. My sister married and works as an electrical engineer in Alabama. She supports Abandoned Little Angels, a Catholic orphanage in Vietnam. There's been no recurrence of the brain tumor.

Xinh. This sister married a man born in North Vietnam. Her husband's family migrated to South Vietnam when Communism took over. When it became apparent that Communism was about to take over South Vietnam, they bought enough boats to get their whole family out. His family first emigrated to New Orleans, and mutual friends introduced him to Xinh. She works as an electrical engineer in Alabama.

Duyên. My youngest sister married a man who also escaped South Vietnam, and was on an island about the same time Loan and I were. As their boat approached that island, the local military shot at them to warn them to turn away. They watched bullets rip through the water alongside their boat. The refugees aboard "punched holes" in the boat to try to sink it. The military allowed those who could swim to come ashore.

They eventually emigrated to the same area of Alabama where we live, and met each other here. She now lives in Georgia with her husband and children.

Thăm. My only brother married a woman born in South Vietnam who emigrated to this area. He works as an electrical engineer in Alabama.

My aunts and uncles and their children

Thang (Dương Mười) and Bé (Cô Mười) with whom I lived in Alabama, moved to Mississippi after my family came to the United States. They worked and retired from the restaurant business there. My aunt has residual damage from the brain surgery.

Their children are all doctors.

Hung, a dentist in Texas.

Minh, an optometrist in Mississippi.

Buu, born on KuKu Island, a dermatological pathologist in Mississippi.

~~~

Ông Bi and Thom (Cô Sáu) stayed in Switzerland where they worked in the restaurant business until they retired. She visited the United States within the last few months to attend a family wedding. Ông Bi died several years ago.

Their daughter Hue, born in the refugee camp, is a pharmacist in Switzerland.

~~~

Mr. and Mrs. VanKirk, our sponsors, have both passed away. Maria attended a Catholic church and served in the Air Force. George attended a Presbyterian church and served in the Navy.

~~~

KuKu Island – Tens of thousands of Vietnamese refugees came through this Indonesian island, with hundreds dying there before they could be relocated.

After the last of the refugees left, the government burned the island to purge it of the diseases harbored there. Now reforested, it is a tourist destination for many former refugees and their families who make pilgrimages there to find the graves of family members.

~~~

Ông Phồn Tam. The boat owner lived in California the last time we heard from him. After my parents came to the United States, they reconnected with him and talked by phone.

I didn't know it at the time, but just before we left, he accepted anyone with two ounces of gold. If my whole family had been there, we could all have gone on the boat together.

~~~

Contact

Website – https://www.TheGroundKisser.com for more pictures, reviews, Thanhisms, and events.

Facebook –
https://www.facebook.com/TheGroundKisser/   For encouragement, reviews, pictures, events, and flag-waving opportunities.

Pinterest
https://www.pinterest.com/lisawsmith57/the-ground-kisser/ - for pictures and information about details mentioned within the book, including the refugee camps, food, and pictures of the countryside.

If you enjoyed the book, please take a minute to leave a review on Amazon.com and let other readers know what you liked about it. Perhaps give a copy to someone in the military, or someone who is facing a difficult circumstance, that they will be encouraged and strengthened for their journey.

Ông Nôi, my paternal grandfather.

Ba, my father.

Mẹ, my mother.

My mother, standing, on her wedding day.

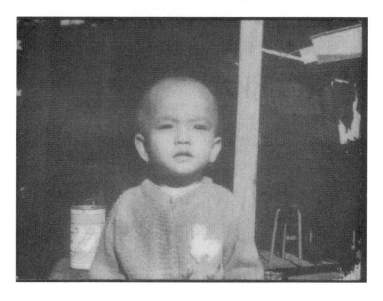

Me, Thanh, as a toddler. Fleishman's yeast in can behind me for our bakery.

Me, Thanh, as a toddler, pictured with an electric fan—a reference to our great wealth.

With some cousins. I am in front wearing shorts.

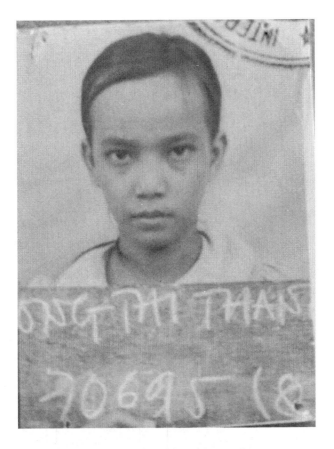

Documentation in the Indonesian refugee camp prior to sponsorship.

Documentation from SeaSweep of immunizations they administered to me.

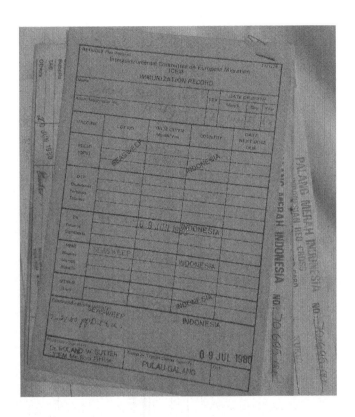

Precious paperwork needed for immigration.

My parents and four remaining siblings in the all-purpose sleeping/eating room a few years after I left. From left to right; Tham, Duyen, Xinh, Thu.

Thanh Duong Boyer with Lisa Worthey Smith

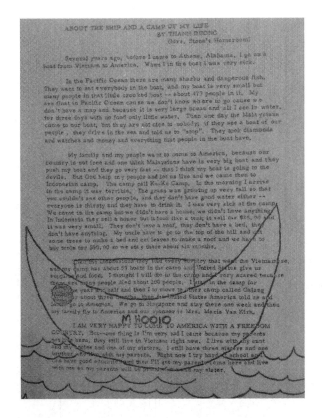

A story I wrote for sixth grade, a few years after I
arrived in Alabama.

The four younger siblings with my maternal grandmother, Ba Ngoai—maker of the best red rice in the world.

My parents and siblings on the lower floor of our home, celebrating the Chinese New Year in the late 1980s.

Thu, Xinh, Duyen, Tham, with an aunt and her son in the background. The son's legs were damaged from polio. They came to the United States a few years after my parents, and now live in Texas.

My sisters and a cousin (in print blouse) upstairs having a party.

Picture of John and me that I sent to my parents by mail. John bought this dress for me.

My wedding day, in a traditional Vietnamese wedding gown.

The only means of communication with my parents and siblings for over a decade. Some of the many letters I received from my family while we waited to be reunited.

When I returned to Vietnam, I brought each of them an

Alabama 1993 National Football Championship tee-shirt. They had no idea what an "Alabama" was, but were pretty sure I lived in one.

Duyen in front of the armoire that held all our clothes. I brought some luxuries including the hairspray and magazines on the tabletop.

Visiting the gravesites of family members.

Snake wine, complete with cobra.

A feast prepared for our visit, served traditional-style on the floor in our upstairs bedroom/eating room.

Typical boats on the Mekong.

The upscale tennis court with concrete pad, next to the cesspool, beside the pigpen, by the public execution area.

John, in the village where my maternal grandparents lived. He was the first American these children ever saw.

My parents' official pictures for immigration to the US.

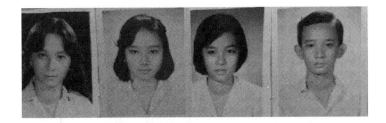

My siblings' immigration pictures.

John met them at the Seattle airport while I waited (eight months pregnant) in Alabama.

Twenty years after the six remaining family members joined us on American soil. Back row from left – my parents, me, Xinh, and Duyen. Front row from left – Thu, Loan, and Tham.

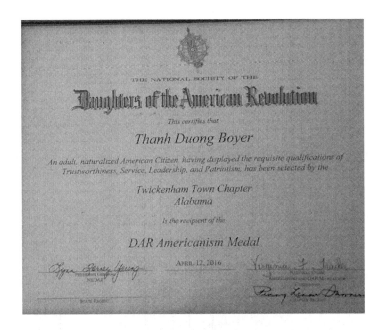

The certificate from DAR awarding me the
National Americanism Medal for "Trustworthiness,
Service, Leadership, and Patriotism."

The National DAR Americanism Medal. The
highest award a nationalized citizen can receive from
DAR.

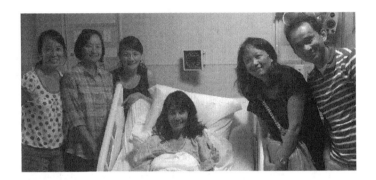

Me just before surgery, surrounded by siblings.

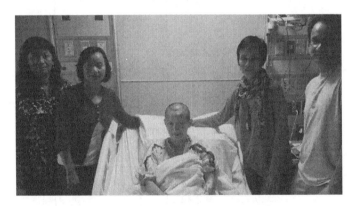

Just three months later, we gathered around our
sister before her brain surgery.

Tumor twins - our first Christmas after surgery.

A sample of "Thanhisms"

I don't want to make the wrong mistake.
Whatever floats your gravy!
I'll be burning the midnight oil at both ends.
Things wouldn't be the same if the foot was on the other side.
Don't forget to flush your teeth.
Floss is more expensive than candies
I know I am stink
I read your mouth.
It starts with "G," as in "D-O-G".
Liar, liar, fire in your pants!
I'm getting on my nerves.
That was a real faux par.
He is not very big for his size.
That really rubbed me off
Listening to rap music will make you steroid
That was the last ditch
Just feed those cats some table craps.
Ignorance is sometimes blister

For more, visit www.TheGroundKisser.com

---

[i] Clodfelter, Michael. *Vietnam in Military Statistics: A History of the Indochina Wars*, 1772-1991. Jefferson, NC: McFarland & Company, Inc. Publishers, 1995, p. 225.

[ii] Neer, Robert M. *Napalm An American Biography*. Cambridge, MA: Harvard University Press, 352. *Nature*. 496 (7443): 29. 2013. doi:10.1038/496029a.

[iii] Oliver, Myrna (8 August 2001). "Duong Van Minh; Last President of S. Vietnam," *Los Angeles Times*. Retrieved 11 October 2009.

[iv] Kiernan, Ben (April 1993). "The Original Cambodian." 242. *New Internationalist*. Retrieved 16 April 2011.

[v] Dean, John Gunther. *Danger Zones: A Diplomat's Fight for America's Interests*. Washington DC: New Academia Publishing, 2009, pp. 109-110.

Endnotes

[vi] Quinn-Judge, Westad, Odd Arne, Sophie. *The Third Indochina War: Conflict Between China, Vietnam and Cambodia, 1972-79*. Routledge, p. 189.

[vii] Heuveline, Patrick (2001). "The Demographic Analysis of Mortality in Cambodia." *In Forced Migration and Mortality*, eds. Holly E. Reed and Charles B. Keely. Washington, D.C.: National Academy Press.

[viii] *Journals of the Continental Congress* (Washington: Government Printing Office, 1907), Vol. VIII, p. 464, June 14, 1777.

[ix] Warner, John (1998). "Senate Concurrent Resolution 61" (PDF). U.S Government Printing Office. Retrieved April 5, 2014. p. 41.